The Female Athlete's Guide:
SPORT NUTRITION 101

Authored by:
Emily R Pappas, MS
Julia Kirkpatrick, MS

© Relentless Athletics, 2019

"Abs are made in the kitchen!"

Raise your hand if you've heard *that* one before. It seems like everytime we scroll through IG we see another fitness model repping a tea detox, a celebrity claiming sugar is evil, or an "influencer" emphasizing the importance of eating clean (how the heck do you scientifically define a "clean" food anyhow…?)

The problem is: these girls are not you. **YOU are an athlete.**

The IG models aren't sprinting up and down the soccer field, spiking the ball on the volleyball court, sinking a game-winning three, or smashing a homerun at the bottom of the 9th.

Unlike you, they don't need stamina to power through a weekend-long tournament or clinic where a scout is eyeing you for a spot on their D1 team next year.

If you want to perform, you have to eat for it.

This nutrition guide isn't about "how to lose 10lbs fast". It won't tell you to eliminate X from your diet or just stop eating at Y time every day.

We created this guide for female athletes like those that train here at Relentless Athletics; female athletes who want science-based nutrition focused on PERFORMANCE - and having a body composition that reflects this success.

Do you want to know what's ACTUALLY created in the kitchen? ATHLETES. Strong, powerful, and incredible female athletes - just like you.

Congrats on taking the first step toward understanding how to fuel your body for performance!

Your coaches, *Emily R Pappas* *Julia J. Kirkpatrick*

Content Guide

Part One: Eat This!
CHAPTER 1: Prioritizing what matters most
Caloric Intake
Macronutrient Ratio 101
Timing
Food Choices and Supplements

CHAPTER 2: The RISKS of under-eating
The Female Athlete Triad & REDS

CHAPTER 3: Get to Know Your Macros
Protein
Carbs
Fats

CHAPTER 4: Eating "CLEAN"?
Defining "clean"
The 80/20 Rule

CHAPTER 5: GAME DAY Nutrition!

Part Two: Drink Up.
CHAPTER 6: HYDRATION GUIDE for the female athlete
How Much Water Should YOU Be Drinking (and When!)
Hydration FAQ

Part Three: MYTHS BUSTED
CHAPTER 7: The biggest food myths and misconceptions

Part Four: Wrapping it up

PART ONE: EAT THIS!

By Emily Pappas, M.S.
w/ Julia Kirkpatrick, M.S.

Chapter 1:
Prioritizing what matters most.

NUTRITION for the female athelte

What actually matters when it comes to your performance:

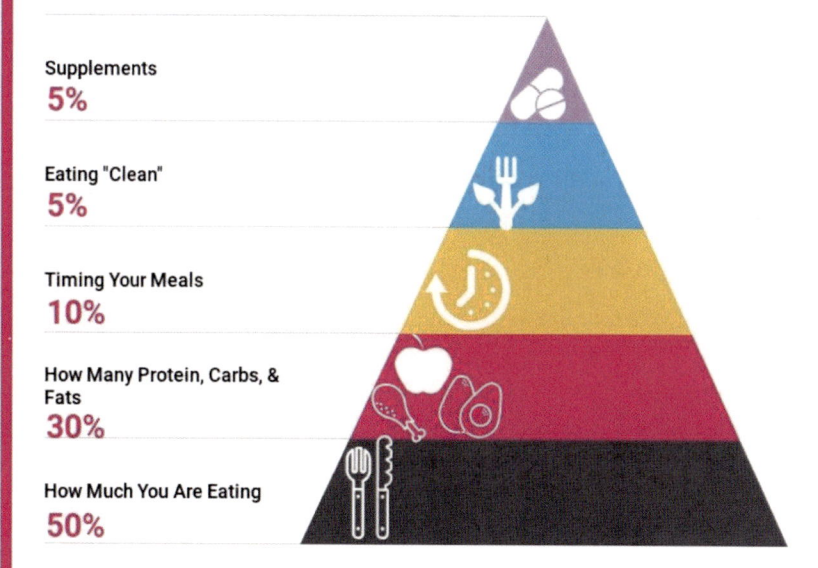

Supplements
5%

Eating "Clean"
5%

Timing Your Meals
10%

How Many Protein, Carbs, & Fats
30%

How Much You Are Eating
50%

"Is Whole Wheat better than White?"

"Is fruit better than bread?"

"Is Halo Top better than Ben & Jerry's?!"

We LOVE talking to athletes about nutrition. We all want to make the best decisions to fuel performance on the court and in the field.

But when we start talking nutrition with female athletes, their first questions always seem to be about whether one choice is 'healthier' than another.

We get it. That's how the food industry has been advertising to us for decades.

But when it comes to science, "clean food" choices should not be the FIRST thing on your mind.

So, before we dive into the virtue of one ice cream brand vs. another...let's talk about how you need to understand the BIG PICTURE first.

Your Nutrient Priorities: What Matters MOST

Instead of obsessing over what's healthier, let's talk about the foundation of your nutrition.

You're an athlete. What you eat literally fuels your kick-ass performance on the field.

Without prioritizing the **amount of food** you eat, and understanding how **carbs, proteins, and fats** differ in how they fuel your performance and recovery, the other details like - when you eat, **choosing "cleaner" food** options, or what supplements you take- **will have LITTLE TO NO an impact** on your goals.

Prioritizing Your Nutrition

When fueling for performance, you need to prioritize **how MUCH energy** you are consuming, and how much of this energy you get from **PROTEIN, CARBS, and FATS.**

Too often, we get caught up in picking the "chick-pea protein pasta" over the grain variation or avoiding food with "added sugar."

And here's the thing…..if you are not eating enough FOOD, or if you are eating enough, but not in the right proportion of PROTEIN, CARBS, or FATS… picking wheat bread over white bread **is going to have 0 effect** on your success as an athlete.

The best way to visualize this is with nutrition priority pyramid.

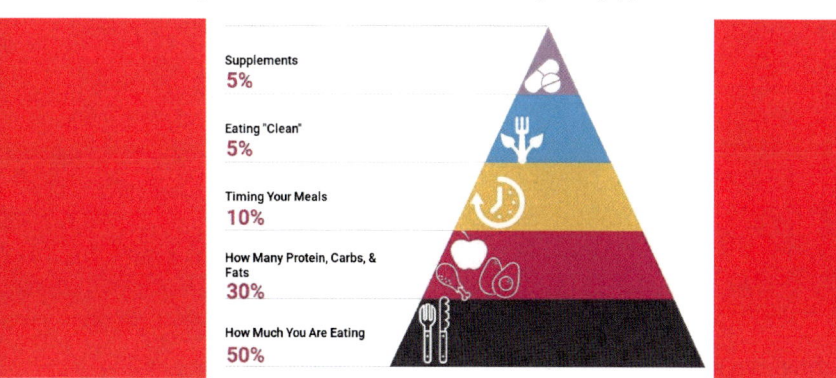

Nutrition Priority Pyramid:
- Supplements 5%
- Eating "Clean" 5%
- Timing Your Meals 10%
- How Many Protein, Carbs, & Fats 30%
- How Much You Are Eating 50%

In this section, we're going to break down:
- **Total Caloric Intake**
- **Your BEST Fat/Carbs/Protein (Macronutrient) Balance**
- **How to Time Your Meals**
- **Eating Clean**
- **And Supplements**

Let's start with what's MOST IMPORTANT. Shall we? ...

Priority #1
THE ENERGY EQUATION

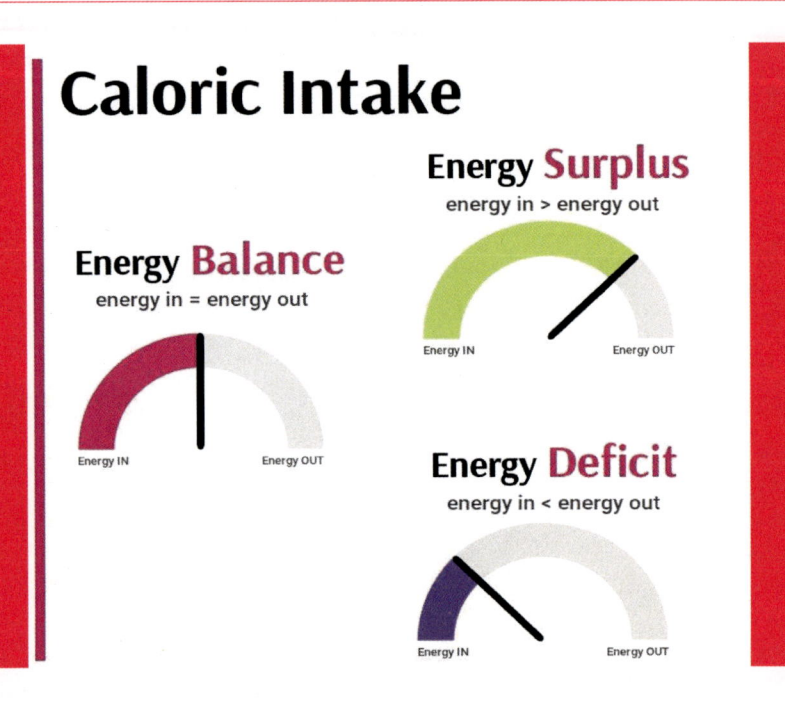

Caloric Intake

Energy Balance
energy in = energy out

Energy Surplus
energy in > energy out

Energy Deficit
energy in < energy out

Before we start talking **"clean" foods**, or the **best pre-game meals**, we need to start with the foundation of your success:

Eating ENOUGH food to meet your performance & recovery needs

Caloric Intake: How MUCH are you eating?

When it comes to fueling your body, half of your success comes down to this:

"Are you eating enough? Are you eating too much?"

It's true. **Caloric intake is the foundation of your success and the #1 priority for female athletes.**

Just eating the **enough** food is going to have the **GREATEST** impact on your performance.

Let me explain…

As a female athlete, you expend a LOT of energy not just during training and on game day, but also on recovery.

Recovery is crucial to performing well. Without it, your body will never be able to respond to your training & adapt to allow for improved future performances..

Think of it this way: **if you decide to put in the work to run a mile you have two options:**

OPTION 1: Run in a circle and end up in the SAME place where you started (no improvements made)

OPTION 2: Run in a straight line and end up in a NEW destination. (destination better athlete!)

We don't know about you, but if we're going to put in the hard work it takes to be a successful female athlete, we want to make sure we end up in a new destination!

Caloric Intake: Performance AND Recovery

Next to sleep, FOOD is the most important factor when it comes to recovery.

If you inadequately fuel your body after hard training, you not only **increase your risk of injury**, but you also risk the chance of **not improving.**

Even worse, if your caloric intake is too low for too long (chronic), you risk **permanent decreases** in your athletic abilities.

You see, when you subject your body to low energy conditions, it must prioritize where the energy goes.

Since your body deems **survival as #1,** your body shuttles the energy to where it is needed MOST: heart, lung, & brain functioning far outweigh your glutes driving your vertical when it comes to staying alive.

If your food intake is chronically low, you risk further issues such as **menstrual dysfunction, poor bone health, and long term hormonal issues** (more on this in a bit).

Too little food = decreased recovery = decreased performance.

BUT WAIT, "if I am under-eating, why the heck aren't I lean? Where are my abs?!"

The body is pretty awesome at this thing called **adaptation**. When we expose our body to periods of *low energy availability*, it adapts!

This adaptation consists of a couple of things like:
- Prioritizing energy towards tasks that are **necessary for survival**
    - → Hello, heart health is way more important than ovulation…
- Reducing energy expended in **NEAT** activities (non-exercise activity thermogenesis)
    - → Find yourself tapping your foot when you are nervous? When your energy intake in chronically low, your body reduces these types of movements to help **conserve energy**!
- Reducing the rate at which fat stores are burned
    - → hey if energy is low, your body wants to make sure the energy it has stored LASTS!

When you are trying to lose a little body fat… ugh this adaptation thing can get frustrating.

BUT evolutionarily, it was pretty damn helpful in making sure we survived when food availability was low.

"But, what does this mean for me as an athlete?"

If you are reducing your intake in an attempt to lose some body fat…understand there is a TIME and PLACE for it!

During your season, your priority should be **performance**. Limiting food (especially carbs) is a recipe for **reduced performance, reduced recovery, and increased risk of injury.**

Fat loss is better achieved in the **OFF SEASON** *(keep your eye out for our next book coming soon!)*

The importance of CONSISTENCY

Ever hear of the term "yo-yo dieting"?

What you do on average is more important than what you do on occasion.

Consider the following example:

Your mom cooked all your meals in high school, but then you go to college and your nutrition drastically changes. You come home from break, look in the mirror and ask yourself, "Does lifting make me bulky???"

Long term results require long term consistent changes. Not just changes when they are most convenient!

Let's do a little math:

Say you need to eat **2,500** calories on average to support sport performance and recovery. Your goals is to maintain your current weight since you're in the middle of your season.

> Monday - Thursday = 2,500 calories
>
> Friday = + 1,000 calories
> Saturday = +1,500
> Sunday = +500
>
> Total surplus = 3,000 calories
>
> 2 months later... + 6-7 pounds!

While you may eat SUPER "clean" Monday through Thursday, the weekend STILL matters. A life with easy access to cafeteria food, late night pizza, snacks, and partying can easily lead to a large weekly surplus of calories. Multiply that over a few weeks and it's not surprising you may have gained a few pounds!

What's the solution to all this?

As the saying goes: **If you fail to plan... plan to fail!**

If you know you have a tournament coming up and not sure what you will be eating, pack your meals! **Your performance and recovery depend on how you fuel your body!**

Trying to adhere to a fat loss diet and know you will be eating out for a family occasion? Look at the menu before hand and figure out a few meal options beforehand. Reduce the stress you have about eating out by going into it with a plan of attack!

Remember: total daily caloric intake is the foundation for our pyramid of nutritional success, but **intake is an average of what your diet looks like consistently!**

Priority #2
THE MACRONUTRIENT RATIO

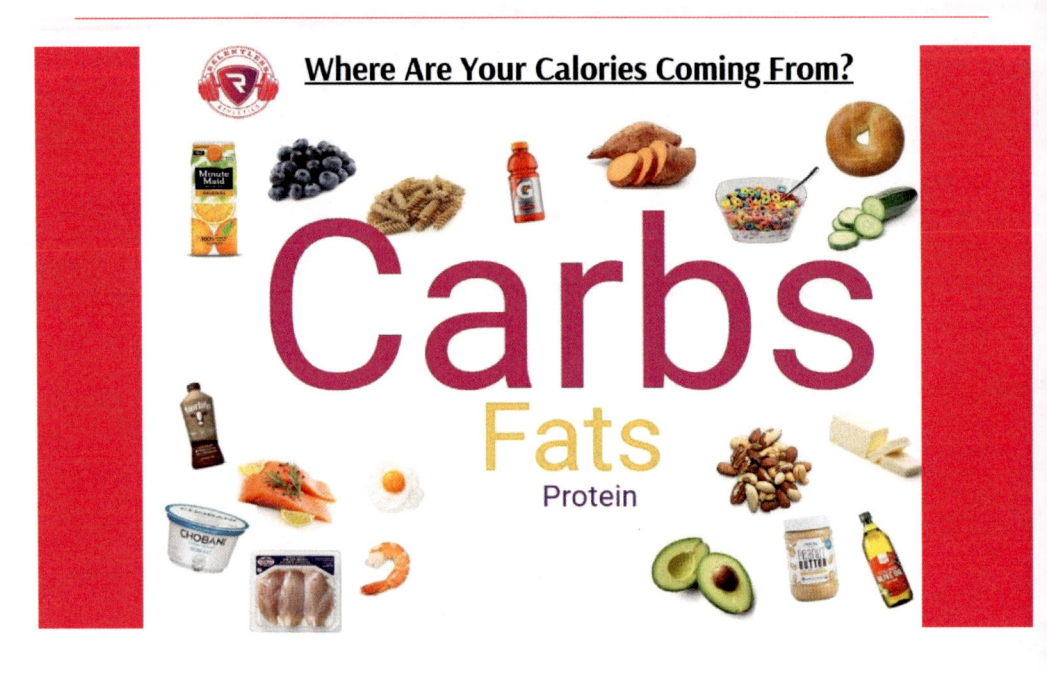

Where Are Your Calories Coming From?

Carbs

Fats

Protein

Now that you're eating enough food to fuel your performance - let's talk about the 'what'.

Your second priority is to consider **where these calories are coming from**, or your **macronutrient ratio**

Macronutrients: What's your ratio?

Eating **enough food** is essential when it comes to the fundamentals of recovery and performance.

But the **ratio of macronutrients** that provides this energy is the second most important factor when it comes to your success as a female athlete.

What are Macronutrients?

Macronutrients are the compounds in your food that provide energy.

These are broken up into three types : **protein, carbs, & fats**

Macro Cheat Sheet

1g Protein = 4 calories
1g Carb = 4 calories
1g Fat = 9 calories

**1g Alcohol= 7 calories

In this chapter, we are going to give you a brief **101 on your macros**

In Chapter 3 we delve into the macro details, helping you understand the different TYPES of each macro your body needs as an athlete. (whole grains vs simple sugars, lean vs fattier meats, fats that are liquid or solid at room temperature)

Protein 101

When protein enters your body, it does one of two things:
1) Act as a **building block** : proteins are composed of amino acids.
    - Amino acids are structural component of muscles, enzymes, & other organs like your skin and nails
2) Act as a **energy source:** protein can be broken down into useable energy (just like a fat or carb).
    - Breaking down protein for energy is COMPLEX & slower as it involves the removal of a nitrogen group

As a female athlete, your goal is to eat enough protein to:
- Minimize **muscle loss**, and
- Optimize **muscle growth**

On average, you should consume **1g of protein per 1lb of body weight every day.**

So, if you're 130lbs, you should be eating 130g of protein every day (or around 5 palm-sized portions).

Where you get this protein is important- but remember this is your 101 guide- head over to chapter 3 for the details

QUICK TIP: There is no benefit to eating extra protein.
More protein does not mean more muscle!

Your body can only grow muscle so fast and it cannot store protein to build muscle later. Rather, surplus amino acids are broken down as an energy source to be used immediately or stored for useable energy for later.

Carbs 101

For female athletes, carbohydrates are the **PREFERRED FUEL** for high-performance.

Carbs are the ONLY macronutrient that can be broken down **glycolytically.** (I.E. VERY FAST)

Conversely, **protein and fats must be broken down aerobically.** (I.E. MORE SLOWLY)

Relying on fats or protein to energize your sprint down the field rather than carbs is a recipe for **slower & poorer performance**.

The amount of carbs you consume should reflect the length and intensity of your training. On average, you should consume between **1-3g of carbs per 1lb of body weight.**

So, if you're 130lbs, you should be eating between 130g and 390g of carbs depending on your training duration & intensity!

On a tournament day with three games, this could look like 12 fist size portions of carbs. On an easy practice day, this could look like 4-5 fist size portions of carbs.

QUICK TIP: Harder training days = more carbs needed

PS...Where your carbs come from matter- we'll dive deeper in chapter 3!

Fats 101

Fats have two primary functions in our body:
1) **A structural component**
    - Fats are found in EVERY SINGLE CELL of our body.
    - They're required to make hormones essential to our health (*especially* hormonal health!).
2) **An energy source**
    - Fats can only be broken down aerobically
    - Fat consumption helps fuel low intensity activity as well as recovery processes

Your body has structural needs. What does that mean? **You NEED to eat at LEAST 20% of your body weight in grams of dietary fat per day for optimal health & recovery!**

If you are 130 lbs, you need a minimum of ~25g of fat. Drop below this level and you are seriously at risk for affecting your body's hormonal health.

Additional fat consumption beyond this minimum helps your body fuel training at lower intensities / longer durations and energize post training recovery.

QUICK TIP: Think of carb and fat intake balancing on a seesaw.

When carbs are higher, fats should be lower. When fats are higher, carbs are lower.

→ **On training days,** carbs are critical for immediate energy & high power outputs. *More carbs mean less fats needed!*

→ **On rest days,** fats help energize your recovery (less intense) and keep you

Priority #3
NUTRIENT TIMING

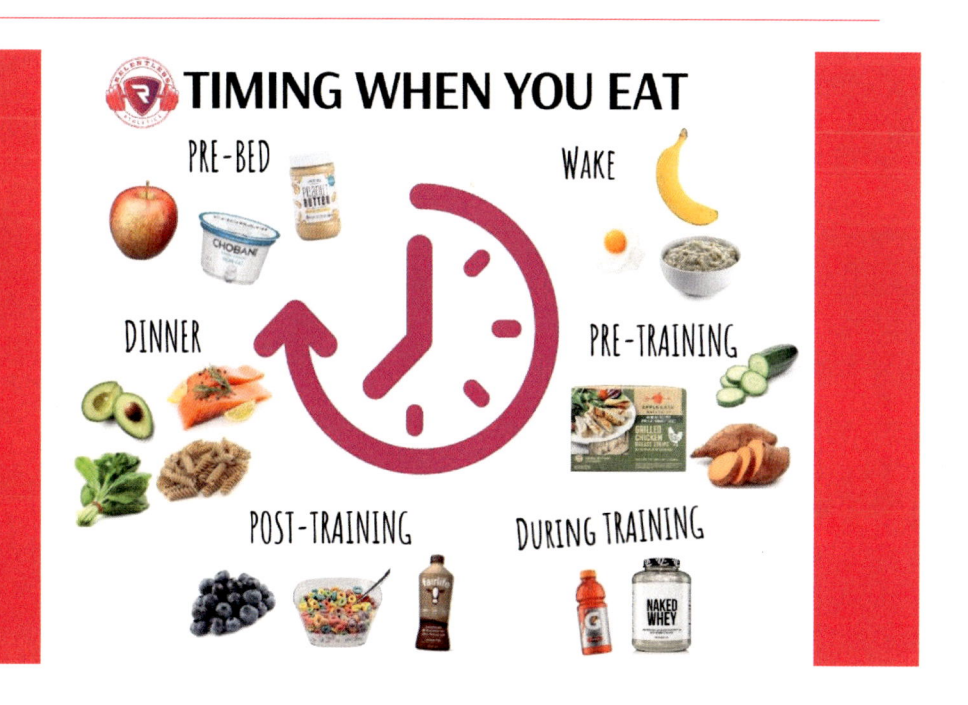

TIMING WHEN YOU EAT

- PRE-BED
- WAKE
- PRE-TRAINING
- DURING TRAINING
- POST-TRAINING
- DINNER

OK, now that you are eating enough food AND eating the right ratio of protein, carbs, and fats on training & rest days, it's time to talk about your third priority:

Nutrient timing or when you are eating your macros before, during, and after your training.

19

Nutrient Timing: WHEN are you eating?

Once you are eating enough protein, carbs, and fats to optimize how you perform and recover, your next priority should be the **TIMING** of these nutrients.

When it comes to fueling your body, the next factor of your success comes down to this:

"When are you fueling your body?"

Are you picking the right fuel around your training to optimize your performance & recovery?

Consider this: Have you ever started a game feeling strong...and by the end, you feel like you **hit a wall.** Those games when you feel like you cannot kick the ball with the same force, or sprint down the court with the same speed as you started the game with?

Yes, this could mean you are not properly conditioned...

But more often than not, it normally comes down to **inadequate fueling before & during your sport training!**

Timing your nutrient consumption can help tremendously when it comes to avoiding that "wall" at the end of your game.

Read on....

Nutrient Timing: how WHEN you eat determines how well you play

You can beat fatigue by

- timing your carb and protein intake
- and limiting you fat intake appropriately around your training.

Again, this **ONLY WORKS IF** you are eating enough carbohydrates overall.

If not, then when you eat isn't going to matter that much...

Here is how it works: Carbohydrates are the ONLY fuel that can break down **glycolytically** (very fast), and power high-intensity activity

If you do not have enough carbs in your bloodstream from your pre-training meal, **your body has to rely on stored carbs** in your muscles and liver (**glycogen**) to energize a sprint down the field or a buzzer-beater three to end the first half of your game.

Here is the thing, within 30-60 min of your activity, **those carbohydrate stores are depleted.**

This leaves you with only stored energy to break down *aerobically* to keep playing. This means **less power output**, and a **slower speed of play.**

Nutrient Timing: how WHEN you eat determines how well you RECOVER.

Timing doesn't just help with performance, **it's essential for recovery.**

The moment your game ends, your recovery begins.

Ensuring your post game meal has both protein and carbohydrates helps make sure

- Your **glycogen stores are replenished** for the next time you play
- Your muscles receive the **building blocks** (protein) and the **energy** (carbs) they need to rebuild

Studies suggest eating protein every 2-4 hours helps make sure your body has the building blocks it needs to keep the recovery process going all day and **reduce muscle loss!**

However, this timing has an impact ONLY IF you are already meeting your body's total protein requirement.

Otherwise, when you eat protein isn't enough to prevent muscle breakdown.

Timing your nutrients is extremely beneficial for high-intensity performance and fast recovery.

But timing ONLY has an impact when you have your NUTRITIONAL BASE INTACT!

You must be eating enough of the right stuff first!

QUICK TIP: your body does not have a protein storage unit!

If your body needs a certain amino acid to help build an enzyme- an amino acid you can't make and haven't eaten in your last meal- your body has to break down its precious muscle!! Less muscle means less power. Less power? You guessed it! You can't perform at your best.

Priority #4
EATING "CLEAN"

Are you eating "clean"?

Caloric intake? Check.

Balanced Macros? Check.

Timing? Check.

Now that you have that down, we can dive into the

Halo Top vs Ben & Jerry's debate.

Lets talk: **Eating "CLEAN"....**

Eating "Clean":

Question: **What is "FOOD COMPOSITION" or "CLEAN" FOOD?**

Answer: **The amount of non-energy providing nutrients present in the foods you choose determines the composition or quality of that food.**

Think vitamins & minerals: these micronutrients are not converted into energy but are still essential to help the thousands of processes and chemical reactions in your body run more *efficiently*.

BUT...**is white bread really *worse* than wheat?**

Well, it really depends if your more important priorities are established first:

1. Eating enough to maintain your weight...
2. AND consuming the RIGHT amounts of proteins, fats, and carbs...
3. AND eating at the right times to optimize performance

If you have these three things locked down, then yes- wheat bread is going to give you a **bigger bang for your buck** when it comes down to vitamins and minerals!

Without a doubt, there is a time and place to discuss the benefits of whole foods and healthy alternatives...**but this conversation should happen AFTER the more important nutrition priorities are established.**

QUICK TIP: Higher refined foods have far less micronutrients than less refined foods.

Think of refined foods as those foods that look LESS like their source

→ BREAD looks a lot less like the grain/flour it comes from

→ While a sweet potato...is clearly the source itself!

Priority #5
SUPPLEMENTS

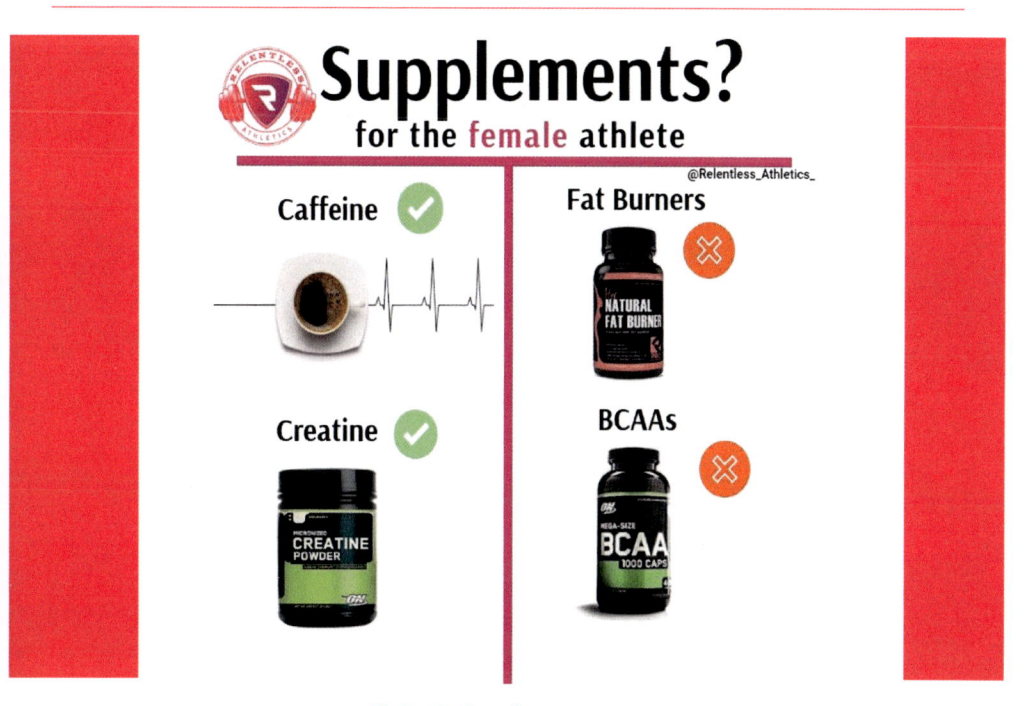

Supplements?
for the female athlete

Caffeine ✓

Fat Burners ✗

Creatine ✓

BCAAs ✗

Caloric intake? Check.

Balanced Macros? Check.

Timing? Check.

"Clean" food choices? Check.

Now let's talk about the *cherry on top* to your nutrition….
SUPPLEMENTS

Supplements:

Supplements are meant to SUPPLEMENT your diet. Meaning, they fill in some of the cracks that might need to be filled from the food choices you make while prioritizing your nutrition pyramid.

But remember, we're talking about *cracks*...not gaps!

If the base of your pyramid isn't strong, if you're running under-fueled, no amount of multivitamin or BCAA supplement is going to help you.

However, if your base is established, supplements can help you take your nutrition to the next level.

For example, maybe you don't spend as much time in the sun during the winter as you do the summer. Maybe you're not consuming enough vitamin D from the dairy and eggs in your diet. Without having the raw material to absorb it, or time to produce it on its own, your body might be vitamin D deficient.

Taking a supplement will help you fill in where your environment and diet lack.

A vitamin D supplement can help provide your body with an essential nutrient needed for strong bones, a robust immune system, and high energy levels!

Just remember, supplements aren't always the same form of vitamin your body produces or absorbs from food. They help fill in the cracks, **but are the LEAST influential** when determining recovery and performance.

So...before you head to GNC, check your grocery list first!

CHAPTER 1 CHEAT SHEET:

Do you want to recover and perform at your highest level?

Then, your nutrition goals as a female athlete comes down to this:

#1- Establish a STRONG BASE FIRST.

Eating enough food is CRUCIAL to your success on and off the field .

If you are not eating enough, you are undoubtedly under-performing and under-recovering as an athlete.

Female athletes must FUEL their success!

#2- Not ALL choices are created equal.

When considering your nutritional choices, remember that not all choices are created equal.

Protein is your building block.

Carbs and fats are your energy source; the amounts you need seesaw depending on the duration & intensity of your activity!

#3- Your nutrition priorities are BUILT on one another.

When you prioritize intake, macronutrient ratio timing, composition, and supplementation...*in that order*...it all works together to fuel your body for success on the field, court, or in the weight room.

If you prioritize the top of your pyramid before the base, you're *wasting your time* and severely cutting your athletic performance short of the success you are capable of achieving!

CHAPTER 1 SOURCES

Aragon, A. A., Schoenfeld, B. J., Wildman, R., Kleiner, S., VanDusseldorp, T., Taylor, L., … Antonio, J. (2017). International society of sports nutrition position stand: diets and body composition. *Journal of the International Society of Sports Nutrition*, *14*(1). https://doi.org/10.1186/s12970-017-0174-y

Beals, K.A., & Manore, M.M. (2002). Disorders of the female athlete triad among collegiate athletes. *International Journal of Sport Nutrition Exercise Metabolism* *12*(3), 281-293.

Bird, S. P. (2013). Sleep, Recovery, and Athletic Performance: A Brief Review and Recommendations. *Strength and Conditioning Journal*, *35*(5), 43-47.

Bray, G. A., & Siri-Tarino, P. W. (2016). The Role of Macronutrient Content in the Diet for Weight Management. *Endocrinology and Metabolism Clinics of North America*, *45*(3), 581–604. https://doi.org/10.1016/j.ecl.2016.04.009

Burke, L. M., Castell, L. M., Casa, D. J., Close, G. L., Costa, R. J. S., Desbrow, B., … Stellingwerff, T. (2019). International Association of Athletics Federations Consensus Statement 2019: Nutrition for Athletics. *International Journal of Sport Nutrition and Exercise Metabolism*, *29*(2), 73–84. https://doi.org/10.1123/ijsnem.2019-0065

Cialdella-Kam, L., & Manore, M. (2009). Macronutrient needs of active individuals: An update. *Nutrition Today*. 43(3), 104-111.

Freeland-Graves, J. H., & Nitzke, S. (2013). Position of the Academy of Nutrition and Dietetics: Total Diet Approach to Healthy Eating. *Journal of the Academy of Nutrition and Dietetics*, *113*(2), 307–317. https://doi.org/10.1016/j.jand.2012.12.013

Ivy, J. L., & Ferguson, L. M. (2010). Optimizing Resistance Exercise Adaptations Through the Timing of Post-Exercise Carbohydrate-Protein Supplementation: *Strength and Conditioning Journal*, *32*(1), 30–36. https://doi.org/10.1519/SSC.0b013e3181c01707

CHAPTER 1 SOURCES

Jeukendrup, A., & Gleeson, M. (2019). *Sports Nutrition (Third Edition)*. Champaign, IL: Human Kinetics

Johnston, B. C., Kanters, S., Bandayrel, K., Wu, P., Naji, F., Siemieniuk, R. A., ... Mills, E. J. (2014). Comparison of Weight Loss Among Named Diet Programs in Overweight and Obese Adults: A Meta-analysis. *JAMA*, *312*(9), 923. https://doi.org/10.1001/jama.2014.10397

Levine, J. A. (2002). Non-exercise activity thermogenesis (NEAT). *Best Practice & Research Clinical Endocrinology & Metabolism*, *16*(4), 679–702. https://doi.org/10.1053/beem.2002.0227

Longland, T.M., S.Y. Oikawa, C.J. Mitchell, M.C. Devries, & S.M. Phillips (2016). Higher compared with lower dietary protein during an energy deficit combined with intense exercise promotes greater lean mass gain and fat mass loss: a randomized trial. *Am. J. Clin. Nutr. 103*(3). 738-746

Schoenfeld, B. J., & Aragon, A. A. (2018). How much protein can the body use in a single meal for muscle-building? Implications for daily protein distribution. *Journal of the International Society of Sports Nutrition*, *15*(1). https://doi.org/10.1186/s12970-018-0215-1

Thomas, D. T., Erdman, K. A., & Burke, L. M. (2016). Position of the Academy of Nutrition and Dietetics, Dietitians of Canada, and the American College of Sports Medicine: Nutrition and Athletic Performance. *Journal of the Academy of Nutrition and Dietetics*, *116*(3), 501-528. https://doi.org/10.1016/j.jand.2015.12.006

Rolls, B.J. (2009). The relationship between dietary energy density and energy intake. *Physiol. Behav. 97*(5). 609-615.

Woolf, K., D.L. LoBuono, & Manore, M.M. (2013). B Vitamins and the Female Athlete. *Nutrition and the Female Athlete: From Research to Practice 2nd Ed.* (pp. 139-182). CRC Press: Boca Raton, FL.

Chapter 2:
The RISKS of under-eating

The long term consequences of eating too little

Females who don't eat enough food for their activity level over a long period of time expose their body to a LOT of unnecessary stress.

Too much stress can lead to:
- Injury
- Sickness
- Loss of Menstruation & decrease in bone density throughout your lifetime
- Mental fatigue
- Decreased coordination & reaction times

Choosing between a sweet potato and a roll at dinner isn't going to change the way you play now or in tomorrow's game **if you aren't eating enough food.**

To play your best, remember, **your caloric intake is your first priority.**

Quick Tip: If your weight tends to drop from the start to the end of your season, this is a sign you are NOT fueling at a level to optimize performance.

Please note: If your goal is to lose body fat, you should NOT attempt this while you are demanding your body to perform its highest during your season. **Cutting calories during your season (high energy demand) is a perfect recipe for poor performance and injuries!**

How do I know if I am eating enough?

There are scientific equations you can find to help you figure out how many calories you need to perform.

But, we aren't going to give them to you.

Why?

These equations give you an ESTIMATE and **calorie counting is not only time consuming, but often inaccurate.**

You see, the nutrition label on the back of your cheerios **can be off by 20%**

Instead of counting calories, you can easily assess if you are eating enough food by watching the scale:

Step on the scale first thing in the morning 2-3x per week.

Track that weight over 3 weeks.

DO NOT worry about daily fluctuations. We are girls, we retain water (thanks hormones), and **fluctuations are normal between 1-3lbs.**

If over the 3 weeks your average is within the normal 1-3 lb fluctuation range, you have met your first nutrient priority!

If over the 3 weeks your average is trending down, you are not meeting your energy requirements.

If over the 3 weeks your average is trending up, you are in a caloric surplus.

The Dangers of Menstrual Abnormalities

If you are experiencing abnormal menstruation patterns (like missing periods, or really LONG cycles (>35 days), this is a HUGE red flag that you could be lacking enough energy.

This is a BIG problem for female athletes!

Studies show that **up to 50% of active female athletes** experience menstrual dysfunction (30% of which are amenorrhoeic or missing their periods all together)!

The cause? **Low energy availability** - I.E. NOT ENOUGH FOOD!

What gives?? Remember, your body is awesome at adapting to its environment in order to **survive.**

When your body is severely undernourished, it takes certain steps to CONSERVE energy for more important body functions (such as your brain and heart's ability to function).

When it comes down to it, **ovulation is definitely not as important as your brain functioning!**

As a result, your body stops energizing ovulation, and you stop getting your period!

Here is the problem: **ovulation is necessary** to keep your hormone levels cycling the way they should not only for a healthy **reproductive system**, but also for your **bone development, energy metabolism, fatigue levels, and your ability to recover from your training!**

The Dangers of RED-S
(Reduced Energy Deficiency in Sport)

When you stop ovulating, you stop getting your period. And missing periods are a BIG warning sign for a deep, underlying issue that, if left unaddressed could have disastrous long-term consequences.

We are talking about Reduced Energy Deficiency in Sport or (RED-s)

RED-s is defined as "the impaired physiological functioning caused by **relative energy deficiency** and includes (but is not limited to) impairments of your: *metabolic rate, menstrual function, bone health, immunity, protein synthesis, and cardiovascular health.*"

Basically, RED-s is an expanded version of the Female Athlete Triad that encompasses **lifelong damage** to your body by:

- disrupting your hormonal balances
- leaving you chronically fatigued
- significantly increasing your recovery time
- And **GREATLY increasing your chance of injury**

Longer recovery means simple injuries like a pulled hammy can take weeks to heal. But it's not just an inconvenience. You see, when you suffer from RED-s you are also at **greater risk for serious injuries like bone fractures and ligament tears**

If you are missing your period you are potentially under-fueling your body. Talk to your doctor about your menstrual disturbances, but keep in mind: **.taking an oral contraceptive WILL NOT help solve the underlying cause of low-energy availability.**

Why Oral Contraceptives are not the solution to missing periods.

If you are amenorrheic or missing periods (and not ovulating), your natural production of hormones like estrogen and progestin are lower.

Remember, your hormones affect other aspects of your body especially your **BONE FORMATION**. For females, our bodies start building bone mass during puberty and peak around the age of 26.

If our hormones are blunted during this developmental period, **we will limit the peak strength of our bones for our entire lives!!!**

To help combat this issues, doctors in the past would prescribe the oral contraceptive pill (OCP) *to put back the missing hormones in amenorrheic females.*

The problem? Taking an OCP to "just put the hormones back in the system" doesn't fix **WHY the problem is happening in the first place.**

Even more, studies on OCP's effects on bone mineral density are not only inconclusive, but also demonstrate **a DECREASE in bone mineral density** when administered to athletes during this pubescent period.

That's right, **the birth control pill can actually DECREASE your bone density** if you take it during your pubescent period.

Why? Because taking an **exogenous hormone blunts your body's natural production** of that hormone!!!

So before you jump on the OCP train, make sure you consider your energy intake.

Want to know more? Check out this article.

QUICK TIP: Getting your period on the pill is NOT your real period.
It's a withdrawal bleed from the hormones your body misses the week you take your "sugar" pills. If you are an athlete who is experiencing an irregular cycle, TALK TO YOUR GYNECOLOGIST and address the root of the problem! Taking a birth control pill is only going to mask the problem and may cause more harm than good!

CHAPTER 2 CHEAT SHEET:

Are you eating ENOUGH FOOD?

Consider these factors!

#1- Monitor your weight

Monitor your weight trends over the course of 3 weeks.

If your average trend decreases greater than the normal 1-3 lb fluctuation, this is a indication that you are under-fueling your body.

Attempting to lose weight during your season is a recipe for poor performance and increased injury risks .

#2- Missing or irregular menstruation is a WARNING SIGN

If your period cycle is >35 days or missing all together, your body could be telling you that your energy expenditure is greater than your energy intake.

This warning sign cannot be ignored as it could indicate a more severe problem like RED-s that can lead to increased injury risks, disrupted bone health, and other metabolic functions that will severely hinder your athletic success.

#3- Oral Contraceptives do not address the root of the problem

If you are missing your period, please remember that oral contraceptives are not addressing the CAUSE of the problem: *low energy availability*

Even worse, taking an OCP during your pubescent period could lead to larger long term issues like decreased bone density and increased injury rates.

If your period is missing or abnormal, talk to your gynecologist and address the possible ROOT of the problem: *not eating enough!*

CHAPTER 2 SOURCES

Huang, Y., Pomeranz, J. L., & Cash, S. B. (2018). Effective National Menu Labeling Requires Accuracy and Enforcement. *Journal of the Academy of Nutrition and Dietetics*, *118*(6), 989-993. https://doi.org/10.1016/j.jand.2018.03.001

Jensky-Squires, N. E., Dieli-Conwright, C. M., Rossuello, A., Erceg, D. N., McCauley, S., & Schroeder, E. T. (2008). Validity and reliability of body composition analysers in children and adults. *The British Journal of Nutrition; Cambridge*, *100*(4), 859-865. http://dx.doi.org/10.1017/S0007114508925460

Mountjoy, M., Sundgot-Borgen, J., Burke, L., Carter, S., Constantini, N., Lebrun, C., . . . Ljungqvist, A. (2014). The IOC consensus statement: Beyond the Female Athlete Triad—Relative Energy Deficiency in Sport (RED-S). *British Journal of Sports Medicine, 48*(7), 491-7.

Polatti, Perotti, Filippa, Gallina, & Nappi. (1995). Bone mass and long-term monophasic oral contraceptive treatment in young women. *Contraception, 51*(4), 221-224.

Stein, C.J., Ackerman, K.E., & Stracciolini, A. (Eds). (2016). The Female Athlete Triad. *The Young Female Athlete* (pp. 57-68). Springer.

Thein-Nissenbaum, J.M., Rauh, M.J., Carr, K.E., Loud, K.J., & McGuine, T.A. (2012). Menstrual Irregularity and Musculoskeletal Injury in Female High School Athletes. *Journal of Athletic Training*, 47(1), 74-82. https://doi.org/10.4085/1062-6050-47.1.74

Weaver, M., Connie, Teegarden, M., Dorothy, Lyle, P., Roseann, Mccabe, D., George, Mccabe, D., Linda, Proulx, M., William, . . . Conrad Johnston, M., C. (2001). Impact of exercise on bone health and contraindication of oral contraceptive use in young women. *Medicine and Science in Sports and Exercise,33*(6), 873-880.

Chapter 3:
Get to know your MACROS

NUTRITION for the female athlete

Where Are Your Calories Coming From?

- Protein 20.00%
- Fats 30.00%
- Carbs 50.00%

Total Intake

Where are YOUR calories coming from?

It all comes down to this:

- What your body needs
- And how certain macronutrients can help fill those needs!

We dove a little into the three macronutrients earlier in this guide.

Now, let's go a little deeper into the role **proteins, carbs, and fats** play in performance, recovery, and adaptation in the life of an athlete.

PROTEIN

Protein is a building block.

This means it is a **STRUCTURAL component** of your muscles, cells, enzymes, and more!

Protein (or the **AMINO ACIDS** that the protein is comprised of) is CRUCIAL for:

- rebuilding muscles after a workout
- cell turnover and regeneration
- producing the enzymes that keep your metabolism running high

If your body is trying to produce an enzyme for your brain to function, but there is not enough amino acids in your diet...you're in trouble.

You see, there is no storage unit in your body for protein except for your own muscle.

When it comes down to survival, your body needs amino acids for enzyme production MUCH MORE than it needs it in your quad muscle.

This means, **if you are not eating enough protein, your body will break down muscle mass** to favor the production of more important things that help you survive.

Not Enough Protein = Loss of Muscle Mass

Not the ideal situation for an athlete who relies on her muscle to perform!

Quick Guide:
PROTEIN
Your Building Block!

NUTRITION for the female athlete

Protein

Lean protein

1 serving = ~25g
1 palm

Chicken breast, lean steaks, Turkey breast, any fish, egg whites, Fat free greek yogurt

Dense protein

Whole eggs*, fattier meats* (ribs, chicken wings, thighs)
Full fat dairy* (yogurt, milk)
*Contains ~1-2 servings fat /& carbs

So...is MORE Protein BETTER?

More protein isn't always better.

As an athlete, you want to consume enough protein to fuel recovery and build muscle mass, but **more won't help you achieve your goals faster.**

In fact, consuming more protein than you need can actually slow your progress!

How?

When you consume EXTRA protein, your body can't store it for structural use. Instead, it will be used as energy.

The problem is this: When your body uses protein for energy, the process is a LOT more complicated than breaking down fats or carbs.

When you use protein for energy, it has to go through multiple steps where certain nitrogen groups are removed so the remaining product can be used for energy in the AEROBIC SYSTEM.

Unfortunately since this process is slower, **protein is NOT the ideal fuel for an athlete that is working at MODERATE to HIGH intensities.**

Simply put, if you are using protein as your energy source, you will not be as explosive, powerful, or fast compared to using carbohydrates as your fuel!

If your body doesn't require that fuel at the moment, the remaining product will be stored for later energy use (just like excess carbs and fats).

When you remove the nitrogen parts of the protein for energy use, they cannot be put back on for later use. This means excess protein will be converted into fat stores for later.

QUICK TIP: Extra protein does NOT mean extra building blocks for later!

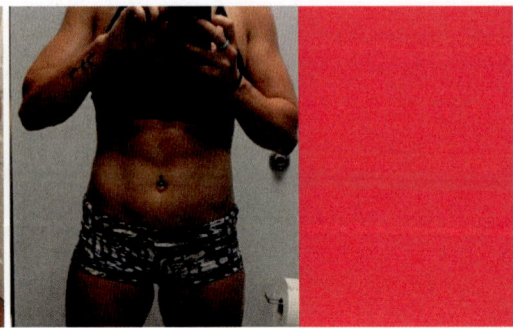

Protein, Muscle Mass, & Peak Performance

To a certain extent, the more muscle mass you have, the higher your metabolic rate.

But what does that really mean? **More Muscle Mass = Higher Metabolic Rate**

When you have more muscle and therefore more strength, the more "work" you can do with any given task.

Think of it as having **a bigger engine to fuel.** And doing more work, or having a bigger engine, requires more energy.

As you build muscle, your body needs more energy to sustain a higher power output and its accompanying physique!

For an athlete who wants to improve performance, her goal should be to optimize her body composition.

This means…**More ACTIVE Mass (muscle) and Less PASSIVE Mass (fat)**

But how does that affect your protein consumption goals?

How Much Protein Do YOU Need?

As a female athlete, your goal is to eat enough protein to MINIMIZE muscle loss and optimize muscle retention and GROWTH.

This means, on average, you should consume **1g of protein per 1 lbs body weight.**

So, if you weigh 130lbs, you should be eating 130g of protein *every day.* This should look like 5-6 palm sized servings of high quality protein per day.

This level of protein is pretty easy to eat without additional supplements, bars, or shakes. Female athletes should aim to eat lean protein ***most of the time*** from sources like:

- Chicken Breast
- Turkey Breast
- Any Fish
- Lean Beefs (90% lean or leaner)

Sources that are less lean and therefore contain more fats/carbs should be consumed ***some of the time*** and include:

- Eggs
- Milk (fat free to 2%)
- Yogurt
- Cheese
- Beef (90% lean or leaner)

Remember foods on this second list **aren't completely lean,** so they also contain energy from other macronutrients like carbs & fats.

Once you consume your set level of protein intake, **there is no real benefit of eating extra.** As we mentioned before, your body can't store protein to use later as a structural building block, it can only be used as energy.

Not all protein sources are created equal!

PROTEIN SOURCES
for the female athlete @relentless_athletics

Most of the time | **Some of the time** | **Limit as treats!**

Protein: it's not all equal!

Look at the back of your peanut butter jar. Most likely, the macro breakdown of this delicious snack will look something like this:

For one serving (equivalent to 2 tablespoons) it's about...

15g of fat
6g of carbs
8g of protein

Total calories: 190

Now, look at the nutrition for your mid-day cheese stick snack:
One cheese stick looks something like:

6g of fat
1g of carb
7g of protein

Total calories: 80

Basically, the same amount of protein which means: Peanut butter is just as good as eating a cheese stick? Right...?

Protein is made up of individual amino acids, which you can think of as Legos. Different Legos can be strung together to make different structures and are in constant flux. As a bonus, the body can create a lot of these individual amino acids on its own: **non-essential amino acids**

However, some of these building blocks must be consumed through your diet because our body cannot create them on its own: **essential amino acids**

Imagine building a Lego house and you're almost done but you're missing one piece to complete the roof on the house. Without this Lego, the structure won't be complete, and you'll be stuck with *a leaky house.*

Choosing the RIGHT protein for your body
3 questions to ask to avoid building a 'leaky roof'!

Q1: Is the protein you are eating high quality?

i.e. – how many **essential** amino acids are in my protein?

High quality proteins have a balanced amino acid profile that matches individual essential amino acids requirements in our body and make it possible to maintain and GROW lean tissue!

Dairy, poultry, and animal products tend to have **HIGH** protein quality: eggs, milk, casein, whey, cheese, meat, fish

Plant-based protein tends to have **LOW** protein quality: nuts, beans, peas, rice, bread, wheat

Q2: Does the protein you are consuming have additional calories that come from other macronutrients? → Protein Density

Let's say you are aiming for 25g of protein in a meal and are choosing between:

25g of protein from a grilled chicken breast ~ **125 calories**

25g of protein from plain almonds ~ **675 calories**

This is almost 5.5 times the number of calories!

While nuts DO contain protein, it is important to remember that protein density (think: how much protein am I consuming relative to the fat and carb content) differs widely among foods.

Q3: Does this protein also provide key nutrients?

Both animal and plant-based proteins offer key vitamins and minerals such as: calcium, iron, vitamin A, riboflavin, niacin, and iron .

A wide variety of food from both plants and animals can help you achieve **all nutrient requirements** !

WHEN Should You Eat Protein?

Your body can't store protein as a building block, and it doesn't really like using it for energy (carbs and fats are way better!).

This means it's a good idea for an athlete to give her body a **consistent supply of protein throughout the day.** Eating 2-4oz of protein (around ½ to 1 palm size serving) every 2-4hrs means you have protein in your bloodstream- ready for your body to use when it needs it!

This balance of "not too much- not too little" not only keeps the protein from being stored as energy, but prevents your body from dipping into muscle stores for its amino acid (lego) needs.

PROTEIN on the go
for the female athlete

@Relentless_Athletics_

easy to grab
- Chobani
- hard-boiled egg
- Mighty Beef Jerky Original

protein bars
- RXBAR
- Quest
- NuGo

protein shakes
- Organic Fuel
- Naked Whey

QUICK TIP: Protein keeps you satiated!

Protein is filling. Eating it throughout the day will ensure you FEEL fueled.

But remember, protein can be used to help build your body more effectively when it's consumed with carbs or fats to help ENERGIZE the building process!

So, each time you have a meal with 2-4oz of protein, it is a good idea to consume it with complex carbs and healthy fats.

This way you KNOW your body not only has the building blocks it needs, but it also has the FUEL required to put those blocks into place!

Speaking of fuel, let's talk about the PREFERRED fuel for athletic performance……

Quick Guide:
CARBS
FAST & EFFICIENT ENERGY

NUTRITION for the female athelte

Carbs

Simple Carbs

Complex Carbs

1 serving = ~25g = 1 fist

SIMPLE
Gatorade, gummy bears
Breakfast cereals
White breads & pastas,
White rice & potatoes

COMPLEX
Oatmeal, quinoa, sweet potatoes
Whole wheat bread & pastas,
Any fruit or berry

CARBS 101

When you perform at high intensities, you need **ENERGY FAST.**

The only macronutrient that can be broken down *anaerobically*, or FAST, to provide energy for high intensity, high velocity performances is carbohydrates.

"But aren't some carbs BAD? What about clean carbs???"

Listen, there is **no such thing** as "bad carbs" or "clean carbs".

Your body only recognizes carbs as energy.

When it comes to your performance & recovery as an athlete, **what matters is how FAST energy enters the bloodstream.**

Carbs are a combination of three different types of sugar:

- Glucose
- Fructose
- Galactose

The rate at which these molecule are digested and how fast they enter the bloodstream depends on

- How MANY molecules of sugar there are
- How they are BONDED together
- And what other NUTRIENTS are present

In the following pages, we're going to look at carbohydrates based on how fast their sugars enter our bloodstream.

Then we will help you understand when consuming those sugars can help you perform as a kick a** female athlete!

CARBS
& your priorities.

CARB SOURCES
for the female athlete

Most of the time | **Some of the time** | **Limit as treats!**

COMPLEX CARBS vs SIMPLE CARBS

"Complex carbs" are **nutrient dense** carbs.

This means they have a lot more to them than just the molecules of glucose, fructose, of galactose. They have a lot of other nutrients that change the way they are digested.

"Simple carbs" are **nutrient poor** carbs.

This means they have not much else to them than the sugar molecules themselves.

Neither simple nor complex carbs are "good" or "bad". They both have their place in fueling your body for peak performance!

The main differences between simple and complex carbs is their rate of energy release:

- Simple carbs are FAST acting because they only have one or two types of sugar (think 'fruit snacks' or 'Powerade')
- Complex carbs are a **combination of multiple sugars (or starches)** that have "more" to them. Not only do they consist of three or more sugars combined, but they also have one KEY ingredient: **FIBER.**

Where Are YOUR Carbs Coming From?

You shouldn't be afraid of carbs. Humans were eating plenty of carbs long before obesity was a thing.

But you have to remember that not all carbs are created equal when we think about the other nutrients they provide. If your diet has 50% of its calories from carbs, you need to choose them in a way that gives you the biggest bang for your buck!

Your performance and appearance will be MUCH DIFFERENT if the majority of your carbs come from **whole food sources** that include fiber, vitamins, and minerals versus from refined carbs found in processed foods and sugar-loaded treats like cakes, cookies, pastries, and candy.

The bulk of your carb intake should come from "whole or complex carbs" such as

- fruits
- vegetables
- legumes
- whole grains
- oats
- potatoes
- beans
- nuts and seeds

Why FIBER Matters

Fiber SLOWS the rate carbohydrates are broken down and pass through your GI tract

When food takes longer to digest, sugar is delivered to your bloodstream more slowly. Slower digestion keeps you feeling **more satiated** for longer AND your **blood sugar remains more constant.**

Even more, fiber helps FEED bacteria that live in your large intestines, leading to improved gut health and nutrient absorption.

QUICK TIP: Beans are a CARB source high in FIBER

When you consider the AMOUNT of protein you get per serving versus the amount of carbohydrates, the amount of carbs is MUCH HIGHER.

Although foods like black beans or chickpeas are commonly thought as "protein", comparing the amount of protein to carbs per serving makes them *primarily a carbohydrate source!* **MYTH BUSTED!!**

SIMPLE CARBS for FAST Energy.

Simple carbs are carbohydrates that digest FAST.

Fast digestion means a SPIKE in blood sugar. This is ideal when your muscles are hungry and need an immediate boost.

Simple carbs aren't complicated: **They're sugar.**

"You're telling me to eat sugar?!"

Newsflash: sugar is not bad. Remember, sugar is the only macronutrient that can be broken down fast! And as an athlete, your body relies on FAST energy to fuel your sprint down the field or the game winning three.

If you find yourself struggling to push through your game or training session without hitting a wall, you might not be getting the fuel you need at the right times.

Sugar is a NECESSARY fuel source for any female athlete who plays high intensity sports!

We are talking to you: volleyball players, soccer players, lacrosse players, field hockey players, tennis players, basketball players, water polo players, swimmers, gymnasts, cheerleaders,......

Simple carbs are NECESSARY for athletes

Quick bursts of energy are *exactly* what the body needs during longer periods of moderate to high intensity training (think your 2hr volleyball practices, all day tournaments, or lifting sessions).

When considering if you need simple carbs, don't just think 'how many minutes' you clock in every week or the "how many calories did you burn" in your session.

Instead, consider:
- Exercise intensity
- Length of each session
- Time between your training sessions

Simple carbs DURING your longer training session are a MUST

After sixty minutes of high intensity training (like your lacrosse game, lifting session, or intense sprint training), you have depleted your main sources of quick energy: the *sugar in your bloodstream and your glycogen stores in your muscles & liver*

At this point in your training your body has two energy options:

- **OPTION ONE:** Turn to fats & protein for energy that is *slower* and will result in *poorer sport performance*
- **OPTION TWO**: Turn to simple sugar added to your bloodstream **DURING** your activity to keep your performance HIGH

The BEST Carbs to Fuel Your Workout
- Keep it SIMPLE!

For QUICK energy **during training,** you need simple carbs. The easiest to digest are liquid simple carbs like

- Sports drinks (Gatorade, Powerade)
- Fruit Juices
- Energy Gels

Because they are easier to absorb, they won't leave you feeling heavy during long, high-intensity sessions. A bag of fruit snacks can also do the trick.

But won't consuming simple carbs during my game make me gain fat???

Short answer- HELL NO.

Long answer- **Simple sugar ingested during activity is preferentially shuttled to your muscle cells** When you exercise, your muscles contract. Muscle contractions help bring your sugar transporters (GLUT4) to your muscle membranes to then bring the sugar in your blood INTO your cells. When you consume sugar, your body also releses **insulin to stimulate GLUT4** to your MUSCLE & FAT cell membranes.

When muscle contractions are high, insulin secretion is LOWER. **This means the sugar you ingest during your training is directed to your muscle!**

What about "BAD" SUGAR?

You might be thinking, "What about BAD sugars? Shouldn't you stay away from foods that have a lot of sugars added to them?" Guess what, your body can't tell the difference between a food's naturally occurring sugars and the sugars added in.

Here is the TRUTH about "Added Sugar":

Added sugars are NOT inherently good or bad. They are just FAST ENERGY with a poor nutrient value.

There is a time and place for sugar without other nutrients. SPECIFICALLY, added sugars are helpful for athletes to ingest large amounts of carbohydrates at a higher rate.

Your body NEEDS a lot of fast energy that does not cause GI disturbances **during:**

- Moderate to high intensity training
- Long training sessions (60+ min)

Consuming energy that lacks other nutrients during this time is completely OK if it helps you consume the energy and if you are choosing nutrient DENSE sugars outside of your training time.

SUGAR FACTS for the female athlete

What is an ADDED SUGAR?
Added or "Free" Sugars are those sugars NOT naturally found in food

ARE ADDED SUGARS "BAD"?
"Natural Sugar" vs "Added Sugar"?
Neither is better or worse!!
More sugar = more energy (& tastiness)

TIMING IS EVERYTHING.
When do you need FAST ENERGY or "added sugar"?

✓ During a long game or practice
✗ During a netflix binge on the couch

DON'T Forget Your GREENS!

We hear it all the time, "eat your veggies!"....but do you know WHY you need them? First, let's consider what veggies are... **Veggies are CARBS!!**

NUTRITION for the female athelte

Greens

1 serving = ~2g carbs
1 fist

Types of Greens:
Spinach, Arugula, Kale, etc
Bell Peppers, Mushrooms, Broccoli,
Cauliflower, Sugar Snap Peas,
Asparagus, Cucumbers, Green beans,
Yellow Squash, Zucchini, Tomatoes

Veggies are CARBS!

Even when you are less active, your body STILL needs carbohydrates to FUNCTION and REBUILD after previous activity

VEGGIES = FIBER

Fiber keeps you feeling FULL and helps push other food through your digestive system

VEGGIES = WATER

Another huge reason vegetables are so satiating is their higher water content. Your body is composed of 50-65% WATER so, your body NEEDS water

Proper hydration is NECESSARY to an athlete's hydration status and electrolyte balance

VEGGIES= VITAMINS & MINERALS

Vitamins and minerals help all the chemical reactions in your body occur FASTER and MORE EFFICIENTLY!

Your metabolism is the SUM of all these reactions!! Therefore, with higher veggie intake, your METABOLISM is going to function that much better!

WHEN Should You Be Eating WHICH Carbohydrates?

CARB TIMING
for the female athlete

During & Post
HARD training

Around training

Further from training

When you are less active...

...your body requires fewer carbohydrates at a given movement for fuel.

During this time, you want to keep the majority of your carbohydrates from **complex sources and veggies!**

Remember: fiber keeps you feeling full and slows the rate sugar enters your blood! This is a good thing. If we bring too much sugar to the blood party when we don't need it, we store it as fat and experience that dreaded *sugar crash*.

Before activity...

...you want to ensure your body is properly equipped to sustain high levels of energy output!

This means a **mixture of COMPLEX and SIMPLE Carbs** depending on how far out you are from training

Remember: carbohydrates are the PREFERRED fuel for performance

During Moderate to High Intensity Activity...

We're talking longer than 1 hour and a pace where it is hard to hold a conversation. This includes moderate to high volume lifts!

Your body is in **desperate need for that fast acting sugar**! After an hour of this type of training, the remaining sugar in your blood from your previous meal and the sugar stored in your muscles will be used up!

This means, now is the IDEAL time to have those yummy **simple carbs**!

"But don't I want to use FAT stores for energy right now? The goal is to burn them off, right?!"

CARBOHYDRATES FUEL PERFORMANCE.

And turning fat stores to useable energy in the body TAKES TIME.

This means when we turn to fat stores during high-intensity activity, we see decreased performance and slower reaction times. Definitely not the ideal tactic when we want to perform our best!

Not to mention, **reduced performance = reduced energy output = less energy required for recovery**

Depriving your body of carbohydrates during your activity not only decreases your ability to perform, but it also decreases the amount of energy your body will need to recover.

Immediately After Activity...

...your muscles are PRIMED to begin the recovery process.

This means we want carbohydrates in your system ASAP!

You want a good **mix of simple and complex carbs**. Simple for our needs RIGHT NOW...and complex to make sure our muscles receive the fuel it will need as recovery continues.

BETWEEN training sessions...

Anytime you have training sessions scheduled less than 24 hrs apart, simple carbs can be beneficial to recovery.

Why?

Simple carbs make sure your muscles receive the sugar they need to **restore glycogen levels**!

Adding them to your post-workout meal will help you bounce back FASTER from the previous session AND better prepare your body for the next

If you train 2x a day, simple carbs are NECESSARY after your first training session to help speed recovery and enhance your next session's performance..

Great simple carbs for post workout include

- White rice
- Pasta
- Breads (especially toast and jam)
- Breakfast Cereals (hello added sugars delivered straight to your hungry muscles!)
- White potatoes

QUICK TIP: Try mixing a sugary breakfast cereal (did someone say fruity pebbles?) with a whey protein shake after your first session on a 2x/day training session!

Talk about an EASY post training meal when you are on the go to your first class after morning lifts!

Further Into Recovery...

It's time to fuel up on high fiber veggies, complex carbs, (and fats).

As you recover from activity, your body needs carbohydrates to fuel the rebuilding process. But it needs fuel at a steady rate.

Further into recovery, your body is also able to take the time to convert your fat stores into energy to use as sustainable recovery fuel.

SUGAR FACTS for the female athelte

Nutrient Dense Sugars

80%

Female athletes should aim for 80% of their carbs to be nutrient dense: all the fiber, vitamins, minerals to help you stay full, fueled, and satiated!

Simple Sugars

20%

Female athletes can fill the remaining 20% with simple sugars that lack the vitamins, minerals, and fiber but still deliver the energy needed for performance and recovery!

How MANY Carbs Should You Be Eating?

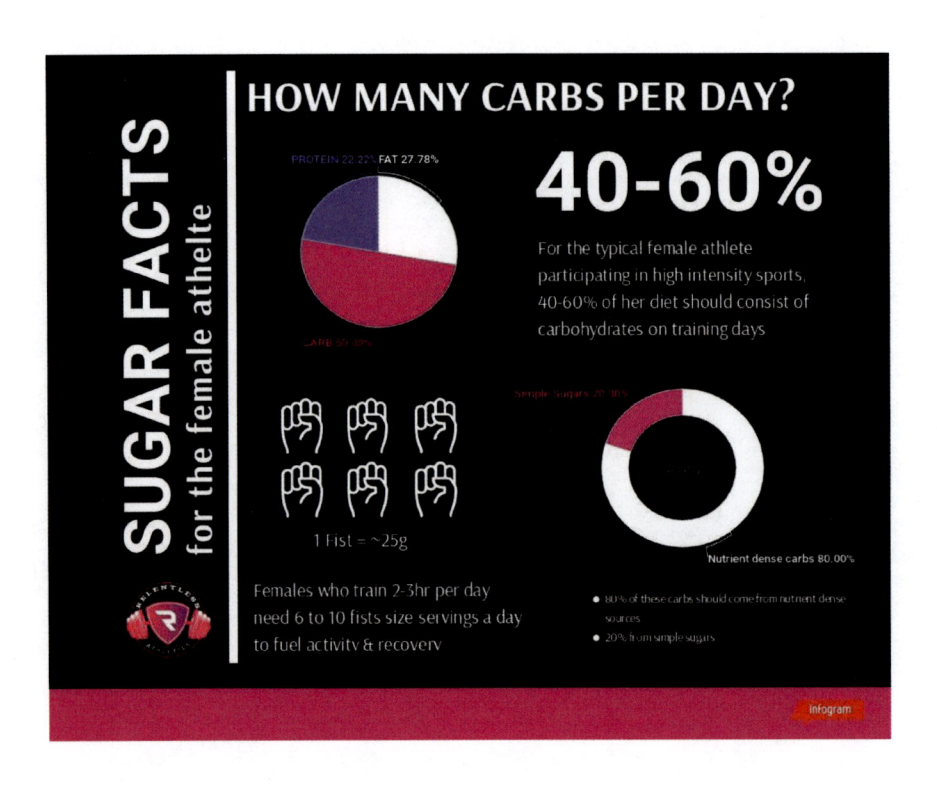

SUGAR FACTS for the female athlete

HOW MANY CARBS PER DAY?

PROTEIN 22.22% FAT 27.78%
CARB 50.00%

40-60%

For the typical female athlete participating in high intensity sports, 40-60% of her diet should consist of carbohydrates on training days

1 Fist = ~25g

Females who train 2-3hr per day need 6 to 10 fists size servings a day to fuel activity & recovery

Simple Sugars 20.30%
Nutrient dense carbs 80.00%

- 80% of these carbs should come from nutrient dense sources
- 20% from simple sugars

Choosing the RIGHT amount of carbs for your activity level

For the female athlete in training, **carbohydrates FUEL performance and recovery.**

Athletes have an energy expenditure much higher than the general population. We recommend almost 40-60% of their daily energy intake from carbohydrates: **think 9-15 fist fulls a day!**

This amount will vary depending on the time, duration, and intensity of your activity

For example, if you are a 150lb female athlete who has a light lifting session followed by a 2 hour skills practice, you probably only need around 8-9 fist fulls

If instead you are playing a full day soccer tournament with 3- 2 hour matches, your carb requirements boost up to around 15-17 fist fulls

But, that's a lot of food!!!

This is where those *fun simple carbs* play a huge role.

Not only are simple carbs such as cereals, white breads, & energy drinks delicious, they are *less filling due to their lack of fiber content.* This means you can increase your carbohydrate intake to meet energy demands without feeling super full.

Remember, **simple carbs are IDEAL for athletes during and immediately after training**

Why Cutting Carbs is NOT the Key to Success!

Unlike the general population, **most female athletes are at <u>high risk of UNDER FUELING!</u>**

This is no surprise given how much of our lives revolve around our physical appearance; yes, Instagram (*hello filters, instagram models, and all the fad diets and detoxes*).

Societal and cultural influences emphasize a certain aesthetic while almost always ignoring the importance of health.

(Oh and they forget to explain how health can lead you towards attaining a bad ass athletic physique!)

This is why MODERATION in your carbohydrate intake is KEY! Remember, there is no EVIL carb. **The real evil is under-fueling in an attempt to achieve a certain look that severely limits your athletic performance!**

Without enough carbohydrates, <u>the female athlete is increasing the amount of STRESS her body is exposed to</u>.

Too much stress?

This leads to **under-performing, break down, injuries, and a decrease in your metabolism**.

When your body is exposed to a caloric deficit over long periods of time, the total amount of calories used by the body during any activity will **decrease**. This is because your metabolism adapts to the restricted energy conditions! Remember, our bodies want to adapt for survival!

QUICK TIP: if you are looking to optimize body composition consider introducing a short term caloric deficit OFF SEASON by incrementally decreasing the number of calories you eat while prioritizing your protein and carb intake to help maintain muscle mass and performance.

Quick Guide:
FATS
The SECRET to the Well-Fueled Athlete

NUTRITION for the female athlete

Fats

1 serving = ~15g = 1 thumb

Nutbutters (peanut, almond, coconut)
Mixed nuts
Avocado
Olive oils, coconut oils

Fats found in other food:

Egg yolks
Fatty meats (ribs, wings, chicken thighs)
Dairy products (yogurt, milk)

Fats provide SLOW RELEASE ENERGY.

Remember how we said CARBS are the PREFERRED FUEL for athletes during activity?

This is because carbohydrates provide our muscles with FAST BURSTS of energy they need to allow our performance levels to remain high!

Further away from activity, however, our body still needs ENERGY to help fuel the recovery process.

The arrival of this recovery fuel to our muscles is not as urgent as it is during activity. As fats are more difficult for your body to digest and take longer to deliver energy to our bodies (via the aerobic energy system), they are the perfect fuel for the recovery process.

Because our bodies need to conserve carbohydrates for sport, FAT is the PREFERRED fuel during RECOVERY!

But there's more to it than recovery. Fats also keep **every** system in our body working at an optimum level!

Fats fuel more than your recovery....

Beyond an energy source, fats are also a structural component of your body!

#1. Fats are building blocks for your hormones!

Fats are essential building blocks for our bodies' hormones…and hormones are our bodies' messengers between systems during recovery.

We need fat for hormone production- especially adiponectin. Adiponectin is a fat-burning hormone that regulates metabolism.

Ironically, not having a high enough intake of unsaturated fats can lead to lower levels of adiponectin- and slow your goals of getting lean!

#2. Fats aid in micronutrient absorption!!

Vitamins A, D, E, and K are fat-soluble. This means your body *requires* fat in order to use them for injury repair, recovery, and growth. You can't absorb them without fat!

#3. Fat helps your cells communicate better!

Fats are part of myelin, a material that wraps around our nerve cells and conduct electrical messages. If your diet is too low on healthy fats, it causes stress to your communication system!

Choosing your Fats:
What's Better? Avocados or eggs?

FAT SOURCES
for the *female* athlete

Most of the time	Some of the time	Limit as treats!

72

"Premium" Fats for the Female Athlete:

Different types of fats are digested differently by our bodies. This means not all fats are best suited for athletic performance and recovery.

For female athletes, we recommend the majority of your fat intake come from mono- and polyunsaturated fats.

Another way to think of these is to think, PREMIUM FAT

You might have heard these fats called "Healthy Fats" or "Unsaturated Fats."

Whatever you'd like to call them, they are an athlete's key for unlocking your body's amazing way of using fats to fuel and recover.

"Premium fats" are nutrient-dense sources of fat that work for the body instead of against.

Favorite Sources of Premium Fats:

- Salmon and Other Fatty Fish
- Grass-Fed Beef
- Olive and Canola Oil
- Oil-Based Salad Dressings
- Walnuts
- Almonds
- Flax and Chia Seeds
- Avocado
- Olives

In MODERATION, we also like:

- Egg Yolks
- Animal Meats
- Coconut Oil
- Butter
- Dairy

QUICK TIP: Premium fats are *usually* liquid at room temperature.

The problem with "Non-Premium" fats

Different types of fats are digested differently by our bodies.

Like we said, **The goal is to have more premium fats (**mon or poly unsaturated fats) than **non-premium fatss (**ie saturated fats butter, animal fats & trans fats found in highly processed foods to maintain shelf life).

But WHY??

Non-premium fats move through the body FASTER than premium fasts

To get more specific, consuming more of these types of fat increases the amount of harmful LDL cholesterol in the bloodstream AND reduces the amount of beneficial HDL cholesterol.

- Think of **LDL** as the type of cholesterol that CLOGS our blood flow through our arteries.
- Think of **HDL** as the type of cholesterol that helps CLEAR OUT particles that clog the blood flow

Moral of the story: Not all fats are created equal because they are not digested & assimilated into our bodies equally!

Fitting FAT into the female athlete's diet

Fats used to be the antagonist of the athletic world. The very name "fat" conjures the opposite of the strong and lean look many of our athletes work to achieve.

Can reducing fats aid in body fat loss? Of course! Remember a caloric deficit is the main factor when trying to lose fat mass. For high-intensity athletes, fats are actually less vital for performance compared to carbs & protein. As such, if you are trying to lose body fat during a structured PHASE of dieting, dropping calories from a reduction in fats may be the way to go.

NOTE: for any female athlete looking to lose body fat, dropping calories DURING your season is the WORST decision you could make for your performance and injury risk. If you are out of season, always make sure you consult a doctor and a sport nutrition professional to help educate your journey of a short 2-3 month diet phase. **Remember, fat loss diets are NOT sustainable long term diets**.

This is because *fat helps you feel full.* And when fats are lacking, you lack that satiated feeling!

When fat is absorbed during digestion, it signals the release of Cholecystokinin or CCK and peptide tyrosine PYY, triggering the feeling of fullness. Without fats, you'll be tempted to snack!

Don't forget, in addition to helping you stay full, dietary fats play a huge role in cell-communication, possess anti-inflammatory properties, and are crucial to the absorption of vitamins. **Chronic diets that are low in fat can lead to depressed weight loss, menstrual dysfunction, thinning of hair, chronic fatigue, an increase in injury rates, and an increase in recovery time.**

CHAPTER 3 CHEAT SHEET:

Knowing your MACRONUTRIENTS

#1- PROTEIN

Protein is a BUILDING BLOCK for your muscles.

Most females need to consume around 5-6 palm sized servings of lean complete protein sources per day

Athletes who do not eat enough protein or protein with ALL amino acids their bodies need will severely LIMIT theri athletic performance

Less muscle = less power = lower performing female athlete.

#2- CABRS

Carbs FUEL your performance and recovery

Choose SIMPLE CARBS for fast energy around your training- ESPECIALLY during training sessions lasting longer than 1 hour or between multiple training sessions in a day

Choose COMPLEX carbs for slower energy that is more nutrient dense further away from your training to decrease the chances of GI distress while increasing the amount of fiber, vitamins, and minerals your body needs

#3- FATS

Fats are SLOW energy that help build your HORMONES & other structures will also providing your body with SLOW energy

Choose fats further away from your training to help keep you satiated and recovering to your highest!

For more guidance on the amount of each macronutrient your body needs depending on your training, check out our Relentless Nutriition Templates!

CHAPTER 3 SOURCES

Armstrong, Lawrence E. (2012). Hydration Biomarkers and Dietary Fluid Consumption of Women. *Journal of the Academy of Nutrition and Dietetics., 112*(7), 1056-1061.

Burke, L., Cox, G., Cummings, N., & Desbrow, B. (2001). Guidelines for daily carbohydrate intake - Do athletes achieve them? *Sports Medicine, 31*(4), 267-299.

Cintineo, H.P, Arent, M.A., Antonio, J. & Arent, S.M. (2018). Effects of Protein Supplementation on Performance and Recovery in Resistance and Endurance Training. *Frontiers in Nutrition. 5*, 83.

Hawley, J., & Leckey, J. (2015). Carbohydrate Dependence During Prolonged, Intense Endurance Exercise. *Sports Medicine, 45*(1), S5-S12.

Karhunen, Juvonen, Huotari, Purhonen, & Herzig. (2008). Effect of protein, fat, carbohydrate and fibre on gastrointestinal peptide release in humans. *Regulatory Peptides, 149*(1), 70-78.

Lambeau, K. V., & McRorie, J. W. (2017). Fiber supplements and clinically proven health benefits: How to recognize and recommend an effective fiber therapy. *Journal of the American Association of Nurse Practitioners*, *29*(4), 216–223. https://doi.org/10.1002/2327-6924.12447

Marra, M. V., & Bailey, R. L. (2018). Position of the Academy of Nutrition and Dietetics: Micronutrient Supplementation. *Journal of the Academy of Nutrition and Dietetics*, *118*(11), 2162–2173. https://doi.org/10.1016/j.jand.2018.07.022

Pochmuller, M., Schwingshackl, L., Colombani, P., Hoffmann, G., & Poechmueller, M. (2016). A systematic review and meta-analysis of carbohydrate benefits associated with randomized controlled competition-based performance trials. *Journal Of The International Society Of Sports Nutrition, 13*(1), 27.

CHAPTER 3 SOURCES

Schoenfeld, B. J., & Aragon, A. A. (2018). How much protein can the body use in a single meal for muscle-building? Implications for daily protein distribution. *Journal of the International Society of Sports Nutrition*, *15*(1). https://doi.org/10.1186/s12970-018-0215-1

Westwater, M. L., Fletcher, P. C., & Ziauddeen, H. (2016). Sugar addiction: the state of the science. *European Journal of Nutrition*, *55*(S2), 55–69. https://doi.org/10.1007/s00394-016-1229-6

Chapter 4: Eating "CLEAN"

Are you eating "clean"?

What does it mean to Eat Clean?

Eating clean is a buzzy catchphrase—referring to food that is "healthy".

What is healthy? A food that promotes your "health" or overall wellness?

When you are on the court and feel the fatigue kicking in, is fruit juice healthy? Well it brings the nutrients your muscles need to help you perform…so sounds like a yes to me!

YAY you heard it here… fruit juice is CLEAN!

When you are on the couch and start to watch One Tree Hill for the 7th time, is fruit juice healthy? Well, it brings your body a lot of extra energy it will not be using and instead store it as fat.

Not that "healthy" right?

CRAP, now fruit juice is UNHEALTHY. Pretty confusing right?

Out of context, labels such as "clean" or "unhealthy" don't hold much merit. Instead of focusing on whether a food is "clean," reframe your focus to what your body needs.

So…big question, does your body ever NEED that pint of Ben & Jerry's?

Changing your perspective on "CLEAN"

When it comes down to it, your body doesn't pass moral judgements on what you eat. **It simply sees everything as a building block or energy source.**

It's crazy to think we associate sugar as always being "bad".

Take, for instance, lets consider that "BAD" SUGAR:

While we rarely associate sugar as "just fast energy"...for a type 2 diabetic about to go into insulin shock, is a soda really "bad"? Or is it a NECESSARY source of fast energy to help prevent a coma?

For a Division 1 field hockey player who is hitting a wall in her game, is a gatorade "bad"? Or is it a NECESSARY source of energy to keep her performance high and carry her team to victory?

Labeling a food as "good" or "clean" doesn't really mean much if you don't consider the situation.

About to sit on the couch and netflix binge? A soda full of fast energy is probably not the best choice, but under a different circumstance it might be just what your body needs!

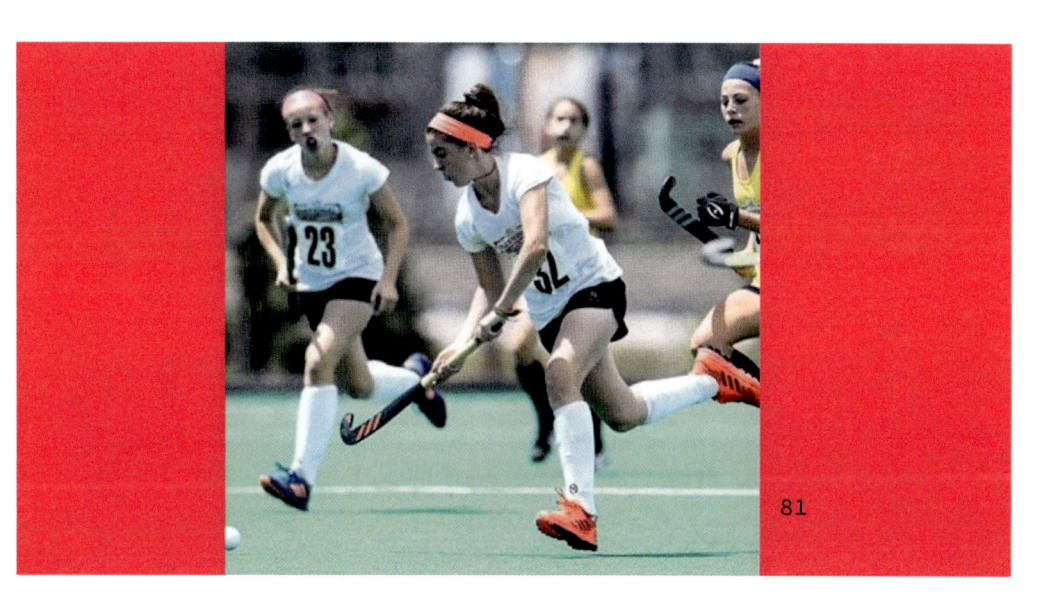

The 80/20 Rule
AKA... "When Can I Eat That Pint of Ice Cream?"

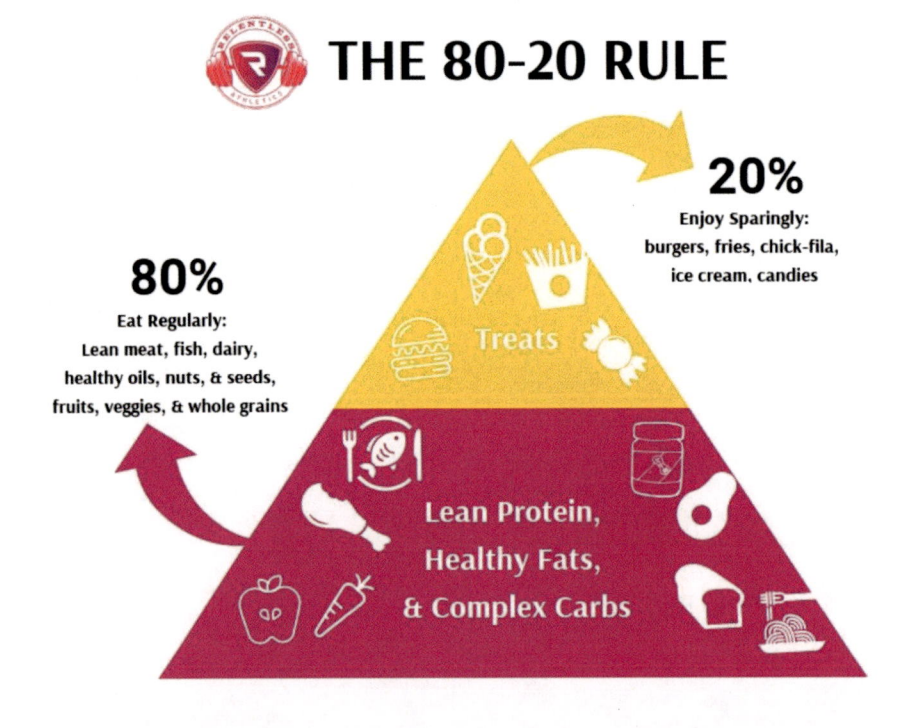

THE 80-20 RULE

20%
Enjoy Sparingly:
burgers, fries, chick-fila, ice cream, candies

80%
Eat Regularly:
Lean meat, fish, dairy, healthy oils, nuts, & seeds, fruits, veggies, & whole grains

Treats

Lean Protein, Healthy Fats, & Complex Carbs

The 80%

80% of your diet should directly serve your health.

This includes all the healthy stuff you've been hearing about all of your life: .fruits, vegetables, whole grains, legumes, fats, and quality protein.

It's SUPER IMPORTANT to focus on this 80% before a practice or game.

Here are some things to keep in mind:

- Opt for **lean sources of protein** (chicken breasts, eggs, salmon) Include **high-fiber complex carbs** (fruits, vegetables, whole grains) for your main energy source on high activity days
- These higher fiber options will keep you feeling full and your muscles energized while providing your body with other vitamins and minerals to function at its highest level!
- Include "healthy fats" for your main energy source on lower activity day.
- Round out your plate with a **handful or two of greens** to add in some crucial micronutrients. Micronutrients may not directly give you energy, but they will help your body break down energy in an efficient manner as you perform and recover.

"CLEAN" SNACK IDEAS

Snack Ideas
for the female athlete on the go

Option 1

Option 2

Option 3

Option 4

The 20%

If 80% of the time you choose foods that are full of fiber, nutrients, and sustainable energy, what you eat for the other 20% will have a much smaller effect on your body.

This 20% should be fuss-free, and can be devoted to food that you simply enjoy—whether or not you view it as "good" or "bad." Still...you might be wondering..

"But, I LOVE ICE CREAM. Is it better for me to choose the "clean" option?? You know, that sugar free stuff?"

As long as 80% of your diet is directly serving your health, this other 20% can be saved up for these types of treats.

What's most important is to be mindful of WHEN you're indulging. A big bowl of chocolate ice cream full of sugars and fats is not a great choice just before bed. But if you're hanging out with some friends after a long week and want a scoop, go for it.

AND ENJOY IT!

One Last Time....There Is No Good or Bad Food!!!

Overall, there is no good or bad food, just better times to eat certain types of food.

If we keep demonizing food, we end up being confused, uneducated, and far more "unhealthy" in the long run.

Overall, having 20% of "unclean" food gives you freedom and will help you keep on track the rest of the time.

Instead of obsessing over every percentage of fat, protein, and carb, you'll find enjoying a burger and fries every now and then is totally fine!!!

In fact, the pleasure of allowing yourself this type of food will more likely HELP you recover from a hard practice or a hard week.

Remember, adaptation comes with quality recovery time! If you are constantly stressing over WHAT to eat and whether it is CLEAN or not, you're holding your body back from optimal recovery.

So, enjoy your food, all 100% of it—it's not only necessary, but your key to optimal performance and pleasure.

CHAPTER 4 CHEAT SHEET:

Follow the 80/20 Rule!

80% of the time choose NUTRIENT DENSE FOOD

Remember food is not CLEAN or DIRTY or GOOD or BAD

Rather food JUST IS. 80% of the time choose food that is NUTRIENT DENSE or food sources that provide many micronutrients (vitamins, minerals, and fiber) in addition to your macronutrients (carbs, proteins, fats)

80% of the time pick foods that give you the biggest bang for your buck

20% of the time eat for PLEASURE!

That's right, if you want ice cream after a week full of hard training and nutritious eating, you can have it!

Ice cream is not BAD- just less dense in nutrients compared to an apple or bowl of oatmeal.

If you eat nutrient dense foods 80% of the time, the other 20% can be filled with more pleasurable foods to help add to your recovery (physically and mentally!)

Chapter 5 :
GAME DAY NUTRITION

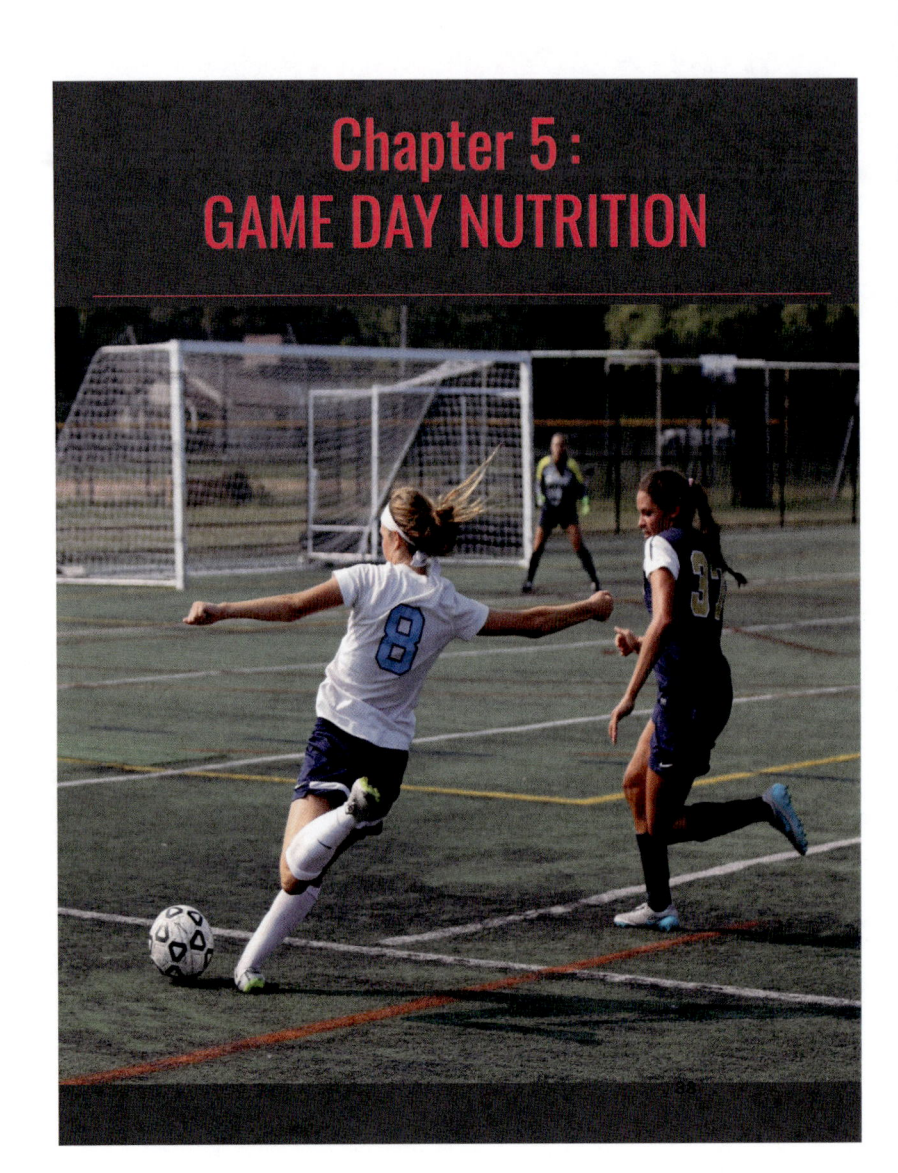

Timing Your Intake

Do you remember our Nutritional Priorities?

#1: Make sure you are eating ENOUGH.

#2: Balance those Macros.

Now- let's dive into #3: Timing Your Food Intake for success on GAME DAY.

The timing of your food MATTERS. It can affect your body composition, performance, and recovery up to 10% in magnitude.

Of course, it is silly to worry about nutrient timing if the other larger priorities (remember: caloric intake = ~50% of your success and macronutrient ratio = ~30%). So, make sure you are focusing on these goals in the right order!

Research shows a relationship between:

The timing of your nutrient intake…

…and the stimulation of protein synthesis, overall reduction of muscle damage, enhancing recovery, and improving body composition.

When thinking about performance and recovery, the timing of your intake BEFORE, DURING, and AFTER your training matters most.

Before the Game:
Fuel For Performance!

NUTRITION 101 for the female athelte

WHAT TO EAT BEFORE YOUR GAME

✓ **COMPLEX CARBS**
SUGAR is the PREFERRED FUEL for high intensity activity

✓ **LEAN PROTEIN**
Protein is a BUILDING block & aids in recovery

✗ **KEEP FATS LOW**
Fats are broken down too SLOWLY for high intensity activity & DELAY DIGESTION

Before Training or Tournament...You Need CARBS!

When fueling before a game, consider what your body NEEDS to allow you to play at your highest level.

Giving your body the energy it needs to FUEL your performance is crucial.

Before a game, you need to give your muscles their preferred energy source.

CARBS ARE PREFERRED ENERGY.

Remember, when you're demanding both SPEED and POWER from your body, you're relying on your ANAEROBIC SYSTEM because it provides energy AS FAST AS POSSIBLE to your muscles.

By choosing a mix of COMPLEX and SIMPLE carbs (such as fruit & bagel or oatmeal with dried fruit), you help provide immediate and sustained energy for your

QUICK TIP: Is your stomach a little queasy before your game? Pick carbs that are a little easier to digest like: toast & jam, cheerios or other grain cereals, or Nutrigrain bars.

Next...Keep Fats LOW.

Fats, though also a source of energy, should be kept to a minimum before heavy activity.

This is because **FATS SLOW DIGESTION**

Because fats are digested slowly, more blood flow will be directed towards your digestive tract and less blood flow directed to your contracting muscles!

Less blood flow at the muscles in your game means less energy + oxygen and a SLOWER performing athlete.

When considering what to eat before your game, focus on prioritizing your energy intake from carbs and minimizing your energy intake from fat (STAY AWAY from fried foods, added oils, full-fat milk, and fatty meats) to ensure your muscles receive the fuel and blood flow they need to perform!

Protein for Recovery

Besides fueling your muscles DURING your game, what you eat helps fuel the recovery process AFTER.

Protein is a BUILDING BLOCK for your muscles.

Having protein prior to your performance ensures your muscles have those building blocks available right when they need them!

Plus, protein helps keep you satiated! Remember, fats help keep you feeling full. With low amounts of fats in your pregame meal, adding protein to the mix can help ensure you don't get hangry-pangs before your warm up even starts!

The Case Against Fasted Training

Studies on female athletes and nutrition are lacking in this industry, but science is catching up with the times! A recent study performed on 43 female athletes around 20 years old, showed that athletes that consumed protein and carbs prior to training showed an <u>increase</u> in fat oxidation after performing high-intensity training compared to athletes who trained fasted.

Simply put, this could mean that eating protein and carbs prior to training will help your body burn fat later!

Remember, body composition is KEY when determining a female athlete's ability to perform. By increasing fat oxidation post exercise, we can improve **the ratio of muscle mass to fat mass** leading to improved performances at a given body weight.

PRE GAME Meal Ideas

(1) LOADED OATMEAL
   Mix 1 cup oatmeal+1 banana, 1 scoop of chocolate whey protein powder +1 small handful of nuts

(2) EGG SAMMY
   1 Whole wheat bagel + 1-2 whole eggs & 2-4 egg whites

(3) CEREAL GODDESS
   Mix 1 cup cheerios + 1 sliced banana + 1 cup low fat Chobani greek yogurt

During Training:
Fueling for Stamina

Keeping Your Training <u>Fuel-ed</u>

When you are playing your game at a HIGH intensity, the stores your muscles rely on for quick energy and the sugar in your blood from your pre-game meal are all used up by the 45-60 min mark.

Without replenishment, you can be CERTAIN your performance is going to diminish.

When carbohydrates are unavailable, your muscles have to rely on fat & protein consumed in your prior meal and stored energy reserves to fuel your game. But remember, these energy sources require the aerobic system and take MUCH longer to give your muscles energy.

The result? *Weaker kicks, slower sprints, and a more fatigued athlete.*

At Relentless, **we call this the dreaded mid game "wall".**

But guess what, you can avoid hitting this wall and turn to another fuel source instead of your fat stores…

Intra-workout carbohydrates!! If you **ingest carbohydrates** during this time your muscles can use the newly ingested sugars from the blood towards the QUICK ENERGY OUTPUT your game requires.

BONUS- add protein for recovery. When you add protein to mix, the carbohydrates act as a shuttle that brings the protein directly into the muscle.

Recovery begins the moment a game ends. The faster your recover, the **more prepared** you are to keep your performance high in the future. By adding protein to the mix, you are **ensuring your muscles have the building blocks** they need as soon as the recovery process kicks into gear.

But won't drinking a shake during my game make me gain fat?

NO!!! Trust us, we get it! It's hard to think about consuming carbs during your game if your mindset is wrapped up in how many calories are you burning!

TURN OFF YOUR FITBIT or other calorie counter and give us a listen…

At the end of the day, remember your **TOTAL caloric intake** is what matters when determining if you gain mass, lose mass, or maintain.

The second most important factor is **how many CARBS, PROTEINS, and FATS** you are eating that help you reach that certain energy intake.

Thirdly, ensuring y**our body has the fuel it needs WHEN it needs to perform** will help ensure you not only PLAY YOUR BEST but also RECOVER OPTIMALLY.

Or think of it this way:

HIGHER PERFORMANCE (more muscles worked at their optimal level for longer) **= LARGER ENERGY OUTPUT** (more energy required to fuel muscle performance and recovery)

Why intra-shakes help your performance & body composition.

Continued performance during a game longer than 1 hour is ONLY possible if you consume a blend of carbohydrates + protein to help provide your muscles the fuel it needs.

If you are worried about your weight, **skipping an intra-workout shake is going to do more harm than good!**

If you are eating a low calorie diet (again, something we do NOT recommend you do during season), you want to do your best to time macronutrients around when your body needs it most!

Remember, **carbs are NECESSARY for performance.** In fact, your muscle contractions make your body highly sensitive to insulin, so that your body secretes less of it. Insulin is a signal to both your muscles and fat cells to store sugar. With less insulin and eager muscles, the sugar you consume goes directly to your working muscles like a direct shuttle!

If you are looking to improve both your performance and body composition, DRINK AN INTRA-WORKOUT SHAKE for games/ training lasting longer than an hour.

If you do, you will IMPROVE your performance, do MORE WORK (expend more energy), and help ensure your body receives the MOST OPTIMAL fuel required for performance.

Remember, a high performing athlete who fuels her body for success is going to have a body composition that reflects it.

Female Athlete Intra Shake Template

Intra-Training
Nutrition for the Female Athlete

For training lasting 1 to 3 hours

Carbs + Protein

Weight	Carbs + Protein
100lbs to 125lbs	20g CHO + 10g PRO
125lbs to 150lbs	35g CHO + 10g PRO
150lbs to 175lbs	50g CHO + 15g PRO
175lbs+	65g CHO + 15g PRO

Make Your Own

Gatorade + Naked Whey

Banana + Chobani

Pre-Made

Core Power, Fairlife, Hershey's

Check out this infographic we made to help you figure out how many grams of carbs & protein you need during your game or training depending on how much you weigh!

If you are taller, more muscular, and weigh more, your body will need more carbs and protein to sustain higher performance outputs. If you are shorter, lighter, or less muscular, you need less!

If making your own shake, we suggest using **WHEY protein** (Naked Whey, About Time, or Earth Fed Muscle are great brands) and simple carb sources like **gatorade powder or fruit juice**. Mix them up or keep them separate, whatever works for you!

If looking for pre-made shakes, our favorite is **FAIRLIFE YUP!** Other notable mentions include Hershey's chocolate milk, Gatorade protein, and Core Power (be sure to check the labels for carbs/protein/fats amounts).

Post Training:
Recover + Adapt FAST

NUTRITION 101 *for the female athlete*

WHAT TO EAT AFTER YOUR GAME

✓ **SIMPLE & COMPLEX CARBS**
Simple to refill your glycogen stores
Complex to energize recovery

✓ **LEAN PROTEIN**
Protein is a BUILDING block for your body

✗ **KEEP FATS LOWER**
Fats delay the digestion & delivery of carbs to your tissues.

Post Training: Let's Talk Stress & Recovery

What you eat AFTER your game is just as important as how you fuel before. But first, you have to understand what your body needs and why.

So- let's break this down:

The body alternates between TWO states: STRESS and RECOVERY.

There are two types of stress—the **physical exertion** required to swing that bat, kick that ball, or lift that weight while you compete AND the psychological or **mental stress** you're under from concentrating on your game.

When you are giving your all for every minute of action, you are **depleting your energy stores** and adding stress.

With every sprint down the court, you are **breaking down some muscle fibers** and adding more stress to your system.

When you strategize how you are going to run your team's final play in the final 30 sec of overtime, you are **burning mental energy.** More stress.

But stress isn't bad!! It is NECESSARY if we want to our bodies to ADAPT and IMPROVE.

If we don't allow our bodies to recover from these stressors, we won't improve.

That makes all that hard effort feel kind of pointless, doesn't it?

Making the switch to RECOVERY

When the game is over, it's time to put an end to the stress and allow your body to recover.

After prioritizing sleep, **what you eat** is the second most important factor that determines how well you can flip the switch to recovery mode.

Ultimately, how well you recover determines how well your body is able to come back and perform again.

When paired with periodized training, **how well you recover determines how well you adapt & improve your performance over time.**

So what should you be eating immediately after a game or training?

The choices you make here should depend on what your body NEEDS.

In recovery, we're focused on two things:

1. **Replenishing** depleted energy stores (glycogen)
2. **Rebuilding** broken down tissue (muscle + energy!)

Bay: 6
WH: 10   Row: 2

BCM 8XG

Title:	One Family's Story: A Primer on Bowen Theory
Cond	Acceptable
User:	bc_list
Station:	ListingStation
Date:	2024-06-07 18:13:16 (UTC)
Account	Books & Etcetera
Orig Loc:	10-2-6
mSKU:	BCM 8XG
SKU:	BCV 0965854027 A
Seq#:	68799
unit_id:	15974775
Width:	0.20 in
Rank:	2,081,356
Cond	ORDERS SHIPPED DAILY! Shelf wear/corner wear. Wear from use. Inscription on flyleaf or inner cover.

BCV 0965854027 A

delist unit# 15974775

XXXXX

68799   0965854027   68799

Step One: Replenish Depleted Energy

Remember how you depleted all of your glycogen stores during your game?

Well, at the end of your game or training session, optimal recovery depends on your ability to REPLENISH those glycogen stores so they can be used again by your muscles in the near future.

In order to refill your muscle glycogen stores, your post workout meal **MUST contain carbohydrates.**

SIMPLE carbohydrates should be consumed immediately after activity when you have another bout of high-intensity activity within the next 24 hours.

COMPLEX carbohydrates should be on your plate to keep you feeling full (thanks, fiber!) and to provide a sustained source of nutrient-dense fuel to provide energy for the *rebuilding process.*

Remember, recovery after your game has two concerns…now that we understand we need carbs to REPLENISH….lets talk *rebuilding?*

Step Two: Eating to Rebuild

During games, your muscles are required to both EXERT and ABSORB a lot of force.

Muscle, tendon, and ligament breakdown occurs when too much force is applied than it has the capacity to absorb.

Protein is a building block for your muscles as well as a structural component for every cell in your body. After a game, eating protein will give your body **the building blocks** it needs to help REBUILD. The faster you rebuild, the more you conquer on the court!

But remember, you cannot rebuild with the building blocks alone.

You need ENERGY to put those blocks in place!

This energy can come from complex carbs or fats, as both provide a steady stream of energy to help your body recover hours after your game! But remember, fats slow digestion!

QUICK TIP: It is a good idea to limit fats in your post game meal.

This helps ensure the carbs you are eating help you replenish your glycogen stores while also energizing the recovery process that helps put those protein building blocks in place!

Putting It All Together

Remember, your game is STRESSFUL. Stress is GOOD when it helps our body ADAPT.

But, we can't adapt and improve without adequate recovery from that stress.

Fueling your body after your game is ESSENTIAL in determining how your body recovers.

With **a meal full of protein, carbs, and a bit of fat,** you will be able to REPLENISH your glycogen stores and REBUILD your body to a stronger, more resilient player!

POST TRAINING MEAL IDEAS

(1) Post Game FAJITAS!
1 palm size chicken + 2 corn tortillas + sprinkle of cheese & ¼ - ½ avocado + veggies = YUM

(2) Chocolate Protein Pancakes
Mix together 1 scoop whey protein + 1 egg + 1/2c oatmeal + 1 banana + almond milk + some chocolate chips :)

(3) After Practice HOAGIE
1 medium roll + 2 slices of american cheese + 3-5 slices of turkey lunch meat + lettuce + tomatoes + light mayo + small sweetened ice tea + medium apple

PROTEIN + CARBS + FATS

+ GREENS =

CHAPTER 5 CHEAT SHEET:

How to eat on GAME DAY

(1) BEFORE YOUR GAME

Prioritize a mix of complex and simple carbs to energize your performance

Add lean protein for your muscle

Limit fats as they delay digestion and cause GI distress

Think: egg whites + bagel + small slice of cheese + banana

(2) DURING YOUR GAMES LONGER THAN 1-1.5HR

Sip on an intra-workout shake that gives you CARBS and PROTEIN (aim for a 2:1 or 3:1 carb to protein ratio) for immediate energy

We love FAIRLIFE YUP! As a easy shake for transport!

(3) AFTER YOUR GAME

Prioritize simple and complex carbs again to boost recovery.

Favor simple carbs if you are playing again in less than 24 hours

Add protein to help your muscles rebuild

Limit fats!

Think: turkey hoagie with light mayo, sweetened ice team, and a small apple!

Chapter 5 SOURCES

Bingham, M. E., Borkan, M. E., & Quatromoni, P. A. (2015). Sports Nutrition Advice for Adolescent Athletes: A Time to Focus on Food. *American Journal of Lifestyle Medicine*, *9*(6), 398–402. https://doi.org/10.1177/1559827615598530

Jeukendrup, A. E. (2017). Periodized Nutrition for Athletes. *Sports Medicine*, *47*(S1), 51–63. https://doi.org/10.1007/s40279-017-0694-2

Kreider, R. B., Almada, A. L., Antonio, J., Broeder, C., Earnest, C., Greenwood, M., ... Ziegenfuss, T. N. (2004). ISSN Exercise & Sport Nutrition Review: Research & Recommendations. *Journal of the International Society of Sports Nutrition*, *1*(1), 1–44. https://doi.org/10.1186/1550-2783-1-1-1

Pihoker, A., Peterjohn, A., Trexler, E., Hirsch, K., Blue, M., Anderson, K., ... Smith-Ryan, A. (2019). The effects of nutrient timing on training adaptations in resistance-trained females. *Journal of Science and Medicine in Sport*, *22*(4), 472-477.

Potgieter, S. (2013). Sport nutrition: A review of the latest guidelines for exercise and sport nutrition from the American College of Sport Nutrition, the International Olympic Committee and the International Society for Sports Nutrition. *South African Journal of Clinical Nutrition*, *26*(1), 6–16. https://doi.org/10.1080/16070658.2013.11734434

Sousa, M., Teixeira, V. H., & Soares, J. (2014). Dietary strategies to recover from exercise-induced muscle damage. *International Journal of Food Sciences & Nutrition*, *65*(2), 151–163. https://doi.org/10.3109/09637486.2013.849662

PART TWO
DRINK UP!

By Julia Kirkpatrick, M.S.

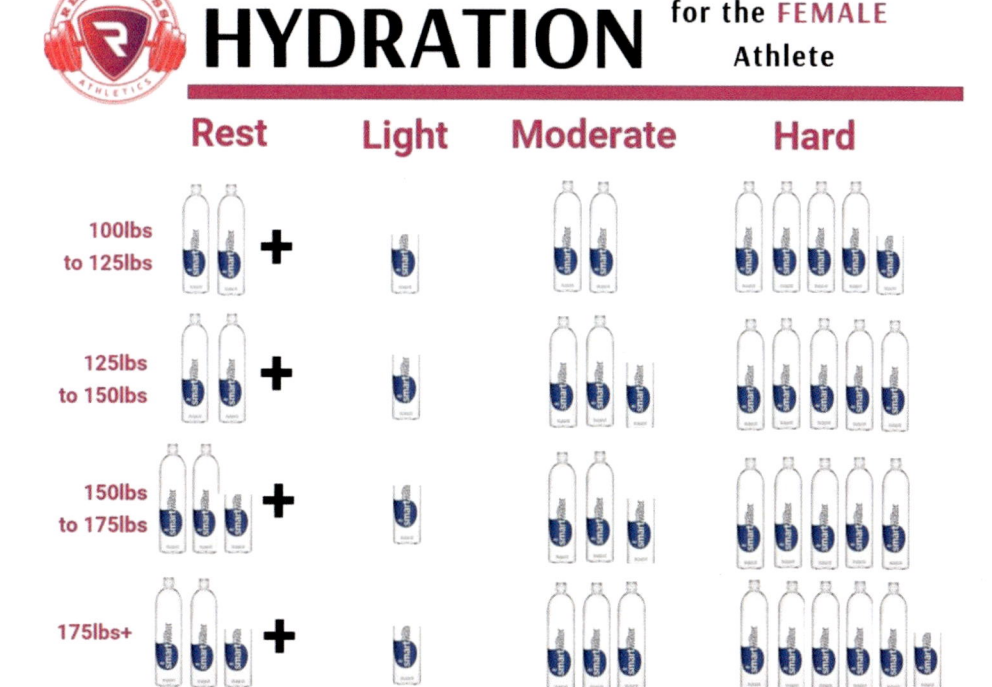

CHAPTER SIX:
Hydration Guide for the Female Athlete

HYDRATION for the FEMALE Athlete

	Rest	Light	Moderate	Hard
100lbs to 125lbs	2 bottles +	1 bottle	2 bottles	4 bottles
125lbs to 150lbs	2 bottles +	1 bottle	2 bottles + 1 small	5 bottles
150lbs to 175lbs	2 bottles + 1 small +	1 bottle	3 bottles	5 bottles
175lbs+	2 bottles + 1 small +	1 bottle	3 bottles	5 bottles + 1 small

Knowing how much water you need isn't as simple as plugging some numbers into a calculator...

Hydration needs can vary athlete to athlete, and even day to day based on things like
- Sweat rate
- Training Environment
- Training Duration

...just to name a few.

As an athlete, you have to prioritize drinking water regularly throughout the day. This can mean consuming 2-5 liters per day!

Pre-Training Hydration: 6-8 ml of fluid per kg of body weight
- Start 2 hours before training/game time
- Preferably drink water with a salty snack
- And remember! Hydration isn't instant- it's a PROCESS!

During Training: 4-6 fl oz of fluid every 15-20 min
- It ALWAYS depends on the individual
- You DON'T need to follow this for training less than 30 min
- For training +1hr, drink a mixture of water, carbohydrates and electrolytes

Post-Training Hydration: REPLACE Lost Water and Sodium
- Hydrate to fit 1.5x your sweat weight within 6 hours after training
- OR 1.5 liter of fluid for each kilogram of body weight lost
- OR 8oz of fluid every 15 minutes until full hydration is reached
- Consume with salty snack

"How does hydration impact my game?"

Hydration is SUPER IMPORTANT to athletic performance!
Dehydration greater than ~2% of body weight can negatively impact:

- blood pressure
- heart rate
- thermoregulation
- brain function
- blood flow
- oxygen delivery

… just to name a few!

"How much water should I drink?"

This one can be tricky.

Why? Well, hydration is dependent on many variables.

But, in general, physicians advise to drink water regularly throughout the day. A sedentary individual (not training or exercising) living in a cool environment needs about 75 fl oz to maintain water balance.

Keep in mind:

1. Hot and humid environments will increase sweat rate more than cool and dry environments!
2. Longer training time will increase hydration needs more than shorter training times
3. *Always* drink BEFORE you feel thirsty! You've already begun to experience dehydration by the time you begin to feel thirsty!
4. Sweat rates are *always* individual - drink according to YOUR needs!

"How will I know when I'm hydrated?"

We know it might sound weird but urine color the most simple way to detect hydration.

It's not always the most accurate...some vitamin supplements can change your urine color. However, your urine color should generally be pale yellow to clear.

"What's better for game time: Water or Sports drinks?"

It depends! If your activity time is over an hour long of high-intensity training, especially when it's hot & humid, you'll be needing plenty of water!

But, it's also recommended that you consume carbohydrates and electrolytes to:

- Help increase rate of water uptake
- Help maintain blood glucose levels —> this will help with performance!
- Help increase the retention of fluid

In high-activity situations, your body could benefit from a liquid form of these - like a sports drink!

CHAPTER 6 CHEAT SHEET:

HYDRATION for the Female Athlete

(1) Keep a water bottle with you always!

The moment you feel thirsty, you are already dehydrated!

Dehydration leads to decreased performance and recovery!

Rather than counting the ounces of water you drink- focus on drinking throughout the day so you never get to the point you feel "thirsty"

This way you ensure you are giving your body the water it needs to be a badass athlete on the field and off!

(2) Add carbohydrates and electrolytes to your water during your long training days

If you are playing your game for longer than an hour with high intensity or in a very hot and humid environment, your body needs more than just water to fuel your success!

By adding some liquid carbohydrates and electrolytes (gatorade or smart water + fruit juice) you help give your body the fuel it needs to perform and the salts it needs to retain the fluids you are drinking!

Chapter 6 Sources

Jeukendrup, A., & Gleeson, M. (2019). *Sports Nutrition (Third Edition)*. Champaign, IL: Human Kinetics

Maughan, R. J., & Shirreffs, S. M. (2010). Development of hydration strategies to optimize performance for athletes in high-intensity sports and in sports with repeated intense efforts: Development of hydration strategies to optimize performance for athletes. *Scandinavian Journal of Medicine & Science in Sports*, *20*, 59–69. https://doi.org/10.1111/j.1600-0838.2010.01191.x

Nuccio, R. P., Barnes, K. A., Carter, J. M., & Baker, L. B. (2017). Fluid Balance in Team Sport Athletes and the Effect of Hypohydration on Cognitive, Technical, and Physical Performance. *Sports Medicine*, *47*(10), 1951–1982. https://doi.org/10.1007/s40279-017-0738-7

PART THREE
The BIGGEST Food Myths BUSTED!

By Emily Pappas, M.S.
& Julia Kirkpatrick, M.S.

Myth #1.
MORE PROTEIN = MORE MUSCLE

Yes, protein is a building block for muscle mass. But, **unless you're supplementing your protein intake with trips to the weight room**, you aren't going to be using all of the extra protein you're taking in.

Your body uses amino acids in protein to repair and boost muscle growth ONLY after you've stimulated your body to NEED to repair it!

Protein isn't a magic fix that automatically converts to muscle after lifting. The key is pairing your protein with the appropriate ENERGY to help put the building blocks in place!

You can pile as many bricks next to a wall as you like, but those bricks won't become a wall unless you use ENERGY to build it.

So what about eating MORE protein than the suggested 1g per lb of BW? ....

Myth #1.
MORE PROTEIN = MORE MUSCLE

When you eat protein, it has three main fates:

- Use it as a BUILDING BLOCK
- Use it as energy (much less efficiently than carbs or fats!)
- Store it as fat

More protein than 1g per lb of body weight is just giving your body MORE of an inefficient energy for your body. Remember, body DOES NOT want to use protein as fuel for high intensity performance as much as it wants to use carbs!!

If you eat MORE protein in favor of carbs, you will have LESS efficient energy to fuel your performance.

If you eat MORE protein in favor of fats, you will have LESS efficient energy to fuel your lower intensity performance and recovery.

If you eat MORE protein but keep your carb and fat intake the same, you are consuming MORE ENERGY than your body needs. Remember, y**our body CANNOT store amino acids for later use.** This means the extra protein will be stored for energy later in the form of fat.

If you eat TOO LITTLE protein,you are severely limiting your ability to build lean mass, improve your performance, and reduce your chances of getting injured.

Protein is necessary for improving your lean body mass and sports performance. Eating MORE PROTEIN for the sake of trying to add *more* muscle is just a waste of your energy consumption.

MYTH BUSTED.

Myth #2
Sugar Addiction is REAL

In today's world, **sugar** is demonized and chastised for many of our health-related problems or extra weight we are carrying around. It feels like everyone – social media, magazines, maybe even your doctor – **is claiming that sugar is addictive.**

Can you really be addicted to sugar?

In order to answer that, we need to understand what an addiction is:

Here's what the science says:

The scientific hypothesis: Sugar addiction may occur through a similar neurobiological mechanism to that of being addicted to drugs. Uh-oh?

BUT there is more you need to know:

There is LITTLE to no evidence that supports sugar addiction in humans!

Myth #2
Sugar Addiction is REAL

Why do we think sugar is the culprit anyhow?

Scientists have hypothesized that there are certain properties of **sugary, fatty, and salty foods** that lead to overindulgence.

However, they have not been able to isolate that sugar is the root cause of 'addictive' behavior.

For example, when you're eating that delicious cake - are you addicted to:

- Sugar itself?
- The taste of sweet food?
- The combination of a high glycemic food paired with fat that makes the whole treat very tasty?
- Is it just a habit? (You enjoy eating something sweet at nighttime because you've been doing it for the past 5 years!)
- Or is it just a *food craving?*

The underlying cause of food "addiction" is likely a MIXTURE of environmental, genetic, and neurobiological factors that still need to be examined!

Here's what the scientists are saying: *The consumption of tasty foods (think cheesy snacks, chips, pizza)* "**has the potential to alter behavior and activate the neural circuitry implicated in food reward**"

So if you think you're addicted to sugar, consider this:

- Sugar is not necessarily the culprit – **there are many <u>other factors to consider</u>**
- "Individual experiences and genetic variation underlie differences in how the brain responds to rewarding properties of food" **MYTH BUSTED.**

MYTH # 3
SUGAR MAKES YOU FAT

Can sugar make you fat? **Yes.** Can fat make you fat? **Yes.** Can vegetables make you fat? **Yes.**

All food is **fuel** for the body to breakdown and use as **energy**.

In fact, during hard training sessions, sugar is a **premium fuel** for female athletes since it provides an efficient source of energy to maintain **high performance**!

Overconsumption of any single food source can lead to excess fat gain, due to a mismatch in energy balance - not sugar!

However, sugar consumption MAY lead to excess calorie intake, since it's often found in super tasty treats that are calorie dense and easy to munch down.

But, is sugar the culprit for excess fat? Not necessarily; remember your <u>nutritional priorities</u> from Chapter 1!

MYTH BUSTED.

SUGAR FACTS for the female athlete

DO CARBS MAKE YOU FAT?
NO.
But too many CALORIES from carbs, protein, or fats do.

CAN AVOIDING SUGAR HELP YOU LOSE FAT?
YES.
When you avoid sugar, you often avoid high calorie foods.

SHOULD AN ATHLETE AVOID SUGAR TO LOSE FAT?
NO.
Avoiding sugar is like avoiding filling your car with high efficiency fuel.

120

MYTH # 4
ORGANIC IS HEALTHIER

What does organic even mean?:

Organic foods are a label for **foods that are produced without the use of :**

- **Antibiotics**
- **Hormones**
- **Synthetic fertilizers or pesticides**
- **Genetic improvements**

Organic foods are NOT treated with substances that could be dangerous to your body in very high amounts.

But does this make them healthier? Well, it depends on what you mean by "healthy". If healthy means **more nutritious,** let's talk about nutrients:

- **MACROnutrients**- gives you energy (carbs, protein, fats)
- **MICROnutrients**- do not provide energy, but are the vitamins and minerals that help your body run more efficiently, and provide numerous health benefits.

Organic foods are NOT more nutritious. MYTH BUSTED.

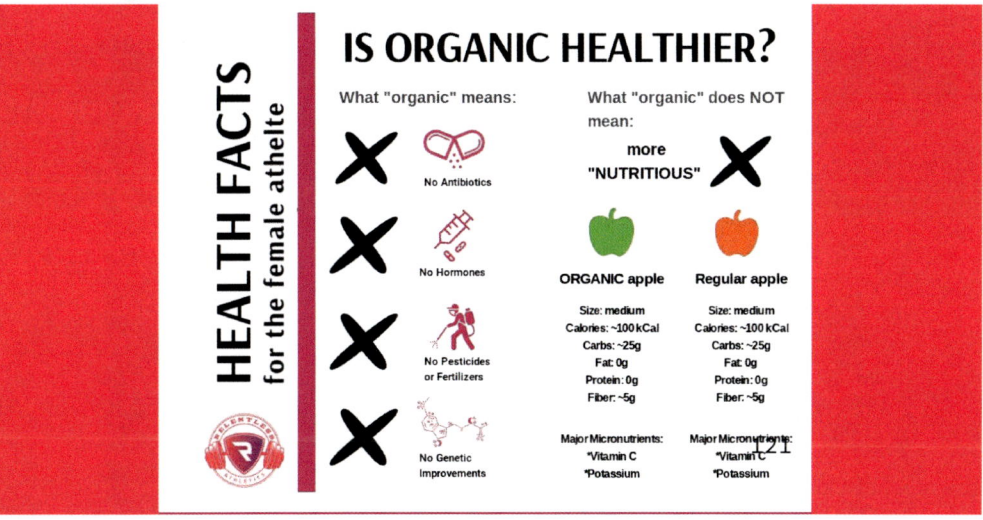

IS ORGANIC HEALTHIER?

HEALTH FACTS for the female athlete

What "organic" means:
- ✗ No Antibiotics
- ✗ No Hormones
- ✗ No Pesticides or Fertilizers
- ✗ No Genetic Improvements

What "organic" does NOT mean:
more "NUTRITIOUS" ✗

ORGANIC apple	Regular apple
Size: medium	Size: medium
Calories: ~100 kCal	Calories: ~100 kCal
Carbs: ~25g	Carbs: ~25g
Fat: 0g	Fat: 0g
Protein: 0g	Protein: 0g
Fiber: ~5g	Fiber: ~5g
Major Micronutrients: *Vitamin C *Potassium	Major Micronutrients: *Vitamin C *Potassium

MYTH # 5
GLUTEN IS BAD

What is gluten anyhow?

- A plant protein
- Found in grains like whey, rye, spelt, and barley
- Helps food maintain its shape acting as a "glue" to hold food together

Where is gluten commonly found? So glad you asked…..

- In foods that are **high calorie & super tasty** (think cookies, & baked goods)
- **Lowly satiating** - food that is equally delicious but not that filling (think white breads, pastas, wraps)

Should you go gluten free? Well if you are trying to reduce your caloric intake, eliminating gluten could help you eat less if you instead choose food with less added sugar & are highly satiating

- Choosing potatoes over white bread
- Choosing brown rice instead of a wrap
- Choosing a bowl of fruit instead of oreos for desert:)

MYTH # 5
GLUTEN IS BAD

Guess what? **"Gluten Free" could also mean MORE calories:**

Thanks to added sugars and fats to help give gluten free foods the same consistency of their gluten containing alternatives

So is gluten GOOD or BAD?

NEITHER!

Gluten is just a protein that provides energy to your body.

Gluten does NOT lead to fat gain. Too many calories from ANY food does.

MYTH BUSTED.

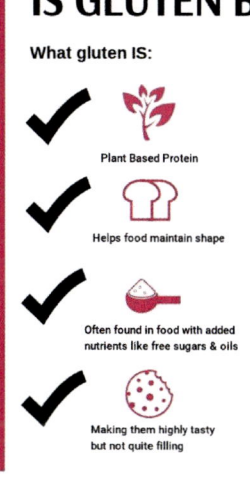

IS GLUTEN BAD?

HEALTH FACTS for the female athelte

What gluten IS:
- ✓ Plant Based Protein
- ✓ Helps food maintain shape
- ✓ Often found in food with added nutrients like free sugars & oils
- ✓ Making them highly tasty but not quite filling

What gluten IS NOT:
- "BAD" or "UNHEALTHY" ✗
- Ideal to eat when you are allergic (celiac) or intolerant ✗
- Eating gluten will cause them discomfort or stomach distress
- ✗ "Gluten Free" does not mean healthier
- ✓ but it COULD mean fewer calories

123

MYTH # 6
SUPPLEMENTS are a MUST

False. Supplements are **supplemental to your diet and NOT intended to act as a replacement for a well-balanced diet!** Plus, not all supplements are created equal!

Should you use them?

It depends. Almost all of your nutritional needs can be satisfied through your everyday diet; however, some supplements can be useful when trying to fuel up quickly and recover on the go!

Supplements that may be useful: caffeine, creatine (monohydrate), carb powders, high-quality protein powders

SKIP THESE: BCAAs & fat burners

But, remember… a strong nutritional foundation must be built first, since supplements are the **'cherry on top', not the main course!** **MYTH BUSTED.**

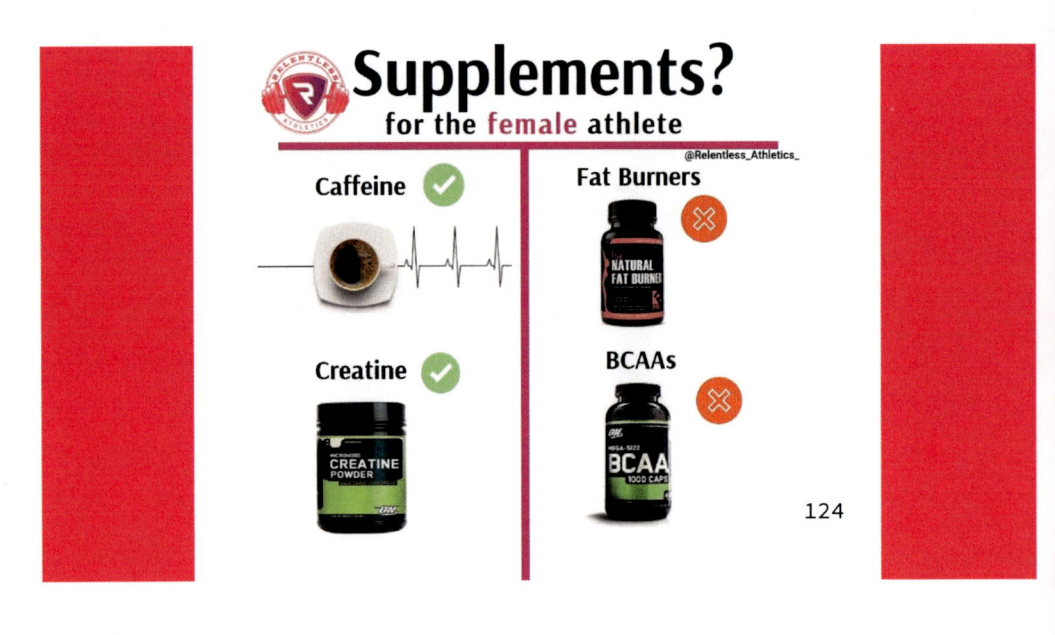

Supplements? for the female athlete

@Relentless_Athletics_

- Caffeine ✓
- Fat Burners ✗
- Creatine ✓
- BCAAs ✗

124

CHAPTER 7 CHEAT SHEET:
MYTHS BUSTED for the Female Athlete

(1)   MYTH 1: MORE PROTEIN for MORE MUSCLE

For the female athlete, she should aim to eat around 1g per lb of body weight to meet her building block needs.

Eating this amount in addition to following a periodized resistance training program will aid in increasing her lean body mass, improving her performance, and decreasing her chance of injury

Any more than this amount will NOT lead to more muscle growth, but rather just extra energy for use or fat storage

(2) MYTH 2: SUGAR ADDICTION IS REAL

There is little to NO evidence revealing sugar addiction is real in humans (sorry IG influencers....)

The underlying cause of feeling like you have a food "addiction" is likely a MIXTURE of environmental, genetic, and neurobiological factors that still need to be examined!

(3) MYTH 3: SUGAR MAKES YOU FAT

Eating more calories (or energy) than you body needs to expend (through activity AND recovery) leads to fat gain or energy storage

This excess energy can come from too many calories from SUGAR, FATS, or PROTEIN.

However, sugar consumption MAY lead to excess calorie intake, since it's often found in super tasty treats that are calorie dense and easy to munch down.

CHAPTER 7 CHEAT SHEET:

MYTHS BUSTED for the Female Athlete

(4) MYTH 4: ORGANIC IS HEALTHIER

Organic foods are NOT treated with substances that <u>could</u> be dangerous to your body in very high amounts.

Organic foods are NOT more "nutritious" meaning they do not have more micro or macro nutrients than their non-organic counterparts!

(5) MYTH 5: GLUTEN IS BAD

Gluten is a plant based protein found in grains. Gluten is often found in tasty foods that provide more calories than you may realize (whats up donuts)

Going gluten free does not make you "healthier"- rather it COULD mean you are eating less calories…..but it could also mean you are eating more thanks to added fats used in gluten-free foods.

(6) MYTH 6: SUPPLEMENTS ARE A MUST

Supplements are meant to "SUPPLEMENT" your diet.

Almost all of your nutritional needs can be satisfied through your everyday diet; however, some supplements can be useful when trying to fuel up quickly and recover on the go!

We recommend athletes look for protein powder supplements (like whey or casein) to help meet their protein needs.

Other supplements such as BCAAs and fat burners are just a waste of money!

Chapter 7 SOURCES

Alonso-Alonso, M., Woods, S. C., Pelchat, M., Grigson, P. S., Stice, E., Farooqi, S., ... Beauchamp, G. K. (2015). Food reward system: current perspectives and future research needs. *Nutrition Reviews,73*(5), 296–307. https://doi.org/10.1093/nutrit/nuv002

Andres, S., Ziegenhagen, R., Trefflich, I., Pevny, S., Schultrich, K., Braun, H.,... Lampen, A. (2017). Creatine and creatine forms intended for sports nutrition. *Molecular Nutrition & Food Research*, *61*(6), 1600772. https://doi.org/10.1002/mnfr.201600772

Arnone, J., & Fitzsimons, V. (2012). Adolescents With Celiac Disease: A Literature Review of the Impact Developmental Tasks Have on Adherence With a Gluten-Free Diet. *Gastroenterology Nursing*, *35*(4), 248–254. https://doi.org/10.1097/SGA.0b013e31825f990c

Astorino, T. A., & Roberson, D. W. (2010). Efficacy of Acute Caffeine Ingestion for Short-term High-Intensity Exercise Performance: A Systematic Review. *Journal of Strength and Conditioning Research, 24*(1), 257-265.

Beaumont, R., Cordery, P., Funnell, M., Mears, S., James, L., & Watson, P. (2017). Chronic ingestion of a low dose of caffeine induces tolerance to the performance benefits of caffeine. *Journal of Sports Sciences, 35*(19), 1920-1927.

Cintineo, H.P, Arent, M.A., Antonio, J. & Arent, S.M. (2018). Effects of Protein Supplementation on Performance and Recovery in Resistance and Endurance Training. *Frontiers in Nutrition. 5*, 83.

Drenowatz, C. (2015). Reciprocal Compensation to Changes in Dietary Intake and Energy Expenditure within the Concept of Energy Balance. *Advances in Nutrition (Bethesda, Md.), 6*(5), 592-9.

Chapter 7 SOURCES

Foster, G., Wyatt, H., Hill, J., Makris, A., Rosenbaum, D., Brill, C., ... Klein, S. (2010). Weight and Metabolic Outcomes After 2 Years on a Low-Carbohydrate Versus Low-Fat Diet. *Obstetrical & Gynecological Survey,65*(12), 769-770.

Hebebrand, J., Albayrak, Ö., Adan, R., Antel, J., Dieguez, C., de Jong, J., ... Dickson, S. L. (2014). "Eating addiction", rather than "food addiction", better captures addictive-like eating behavior. *Neuroscience & Biobehavioral Reviews, 47*, 295–306. https://doi.org/10.1016/j.neubiorev.2014.08.016

Jeukendrup, A. E. (2017). Periodized Nutrition for Athletes. *Sports Medicine, 47*(S1), 51–63. https://doi.org/10.1007/s40279-017-0694-2

Kerksick, C., Wilborn, C., Roberts, M., Smith-Ryan, A., Kleiner, S., Jager, R., ... Jaeger, C. (2018). ISSN exercise & sports nutrition review update: Research & recommendations. *Journal of The International Society Of Sports Nutrition, 15*(1), 1-57.

Lammers, K. M., Herrera, M. G., & Dodero, V. I. (2018). Translational Chemistry Meets Gluten Related Disorders. *ChemistryOpen, 7*(3), 217-232. https://doi.org/10.1002/open.201700197

Long, C. G., Blundell, J. E., & Finlayson, G. (2015). A Systematic Review of the Application And Correlates of YFAS-Diagnosed 'Food Addiction" in Humans: Are Eating-Related "Addictions" a Cause for Concern or Empty Concepts?'" *Obesity Facts, 8*(6), 386–401. https://doi.org/10.1159/000442403

Maughan, R., Burke, L., Dvorak, J., Larson-Meyer, D., Peeling, P., Phillips, S., ... Engebretsen, L. (2018). IOC consensus statement: Dietary supplements and the high-performance athlete. *British Journal of Sports Medicine, 52*(7), 439-455.

Chapter 7 SOURCES

Singh, H., & MacRitchie, F. (2001). Application of Polymer Science to Properties of Gluten. *Journal of Cereal Science*, *33*(3), 231–243
https://doi.org/10.1006/jcrs.2000.0360

Smith-Spangler, C., Brandeau, M. L., Hunter, G. E., Bavinger, J. C., Pearson, M., Eschbach, P. J., … Bravata, D. M. (2012). Are Organic Foods Safer or Healthier Than Conventional Alternatives?: A Systematic Review. *Annals of Internal Medicine*, *157*(5), 348. https://doi.org/10.7326/0003-4819-157-5-201209040-00007

Westwater, M. L., Fletcher, P. C., & Ziauddeen, H. (2016). Sugar addiction: the state of the science. *European Journal of Nutrition*, *55*(S2), 55–69.
https://doi.org/10.1007/s00394-016-1229

Wolfe, R. (2017). Branched-chain amino acids and muscle protein synthesis in humans: Myth or reality? *Journal of the International Society of Sports Nutrition, 14*(1), 30.

PART FOUR:
Wrap it Up.
So...What Will YOU Do Next?
By Emily Pappas, M.S.
& Julia Kirkpatrick, M.S.

Let us ask you something...

When you're on the field do you feel like you should do *more*-but can't?

What would last season look like with better nutrition?

How would your season have gone had you followed the nutrient priorities we have outlined in this book?

How much more power would you have to:

>....perform higher and for longer each game?

>....recover & adapt to the demands of your training?

So let us ask...how committed are you now?

In this guide, we have given you everything you need to create your own success.

We've broken down the REAL NUTRITIONAL PRIORITIES successful athletes need. We've talked macros, timing, hydration, and the biggest food myths holding women back from their ultimate performance level.

So, are you committed to playing at your peak? If so, we can help.

How? By supporting you.

Here's the truth:

You know success as an athlete is 80% you...and 20% *your team.*

Your Success is YOUR TEAM

Your team is more than your friends on your field. Your team is your coaches, your trainers, the heroes who inspire you. Your team is the people you call on to stay strong while you achieve an 'impossible' goal one after another.

You wouldn't hit the weight room without a coach… or *at least a program* right?

Why?

Without a plan, you end up putting in a lot work, with zero return on your investment.

Nutrition works the same way!

Think of this book as your program to fuel your body (the right way) this season.

The RIGHT nutrition plan EDUCATES you on the why:

We get it. This ebook is not a book that tells you "eat this, not that"

And that's the point!

We want you to help TEACH you what actually matters when it comes to fueling as an athlete.

The problem is: not everyone is a self-learner. And we get it!

Even more, the information in this book is detailed but the execution isn't personalized to your situation.

If you need personalized help, we can help!

But first, we need to know who are we really talking to!

If you're struggling to kick-start your metabolism, knowing you need to eat more but can't make the change...

If you have dietary restrictions and can't seem to build muscle mass...

If you've chosen a vegetarian or vegan lifestyle, but find yourself just eating carbs and falling short on results...

If you're stuck on the bench recovering from an injury and need to eat in a way to get you back on the field fast...

We're here for you.

Our goal at Relentless Athletics is to give female athletes *everything* they need to perform at their best *now*- and *for their entire career.*

Let's Talk!

You've read this giant eBook. You're serious about your sport; we're serious, too. If you have questions, or want to take your sports performance to the next level but don't know the next steps...

Feel free to schedule a one-on-one nutrition consult by clicking [here.](#)

In your personalized nutrition consult we go over your current intake and help devise a individualized program for you to better meet the nutrient priorities in this book.

Not ready to leap straight into personalized coaching? That's cool, too!

We created a series of DIY nutrition templates to fuel your nutrition needs as a female athlete.

These templates feature done-for-you nutrition solutions that work EVEN if you're living dorm-style without a kitchen. Each template is easy to follow and accounts for body weight, training level of athleticism, training length, and intensity.

Everything is 'plug and play'. Download the nutrition templates here.

One last thing before we sign off.

Being a badass female athlete is no small achievement.

You've balled, batted, and battled your way through old-school social norms to show the world your warrior spirit. You've trained hard, scored harder, and broken everyone's expectations.

If you want to PREFORM...

If you want to RECOVER...

If you want a BODY COMPOSITION that reflects YOUR HARD WORK...

This book has all of the principles you need to get where you want to go.

We're here to back you up. Anytime you have a question about nutrition, you can schedule a [consult call here](#) and we'll talk you through it!

Your coaches,

Emily R Pappas   *Julia J. Kirkpatrick*

About the authors

Who is Emily?

Emily's passion is helping females become lifelong athletes. Her company Relentless Athletics, specializes in the development of female athletes through strength training, sports nutrition, and sports injury rehabilitation

Located in Hatfield, PA, Emily and her team help develop female athletes from youth to the collegiate & professional level.

Emily Pappas holds a MS in Exercise Physiology, a BS in Biological Sciences with a concentration in biochemistry, and is an adjunct instructor at Temple University instructing a course on the science and socio historical implications behind female athlete development at Temple University.

Who is Julia?

Julia's passion is bringing an evidence-based approach to sports training and nutrition practice. Her time spent as a D1 strength coach highlighted a gap that needed to be filled – specifically for female athletes. Relentless Athletics provides the resources for female athletes to learn, develop, and get strong!

Julia holds a MS in Applied Sports Science & Coach Education and BS in Kinesiology (Exercise/Sports Science).

Made in the USA
Middletown, DE
28 August 2019